SYMBOLS AND GRAPIC REPRESENTATIONS IN INDIAN INSCRIPTIONS

SYMBOLS AND GRAPIC REPRESENTATIONS IN INDIAN INSCRIPTIONS

H. SARKAR
B.M. PANDE

Aryan Books International
New Delhi

Symbols and Graphic Representations in Indian Inscriptions

ISBN: 978-81-7305-163-0

First Published: 1999

Reprinted: 2023

Published by:

Aryan Books International
Pooja Apartments, 4B, Ansari Road, New Delhi-110002 (India)
Tel.: 23287589, 23255799; Fax: 91-11-23270385
E-mail: aryanbooks@gmail.com
www.aryanbooks.com

Printed in India

PREFACE

This monograph is about symbols and graphic representations occurring in Indian inscriptions, both Sanskrit and Dravidian. These representations, whether symbols or graphic have usually not received the attention they deserve with the exception of some symbols like the *svastika* or the one for *Oṁ* or *siddhaṁ*. In contrast, symbols in coins, particularly the early ones, as well as symbols and motifs in art have been studied and analysed in great detail. This is natural since in an inscription the text is primary and the symbol or graphic representation occurring in an inscription is generally considered to be of little or no importance. We therefore started collecting examples of symbols and graphic representations in inscriptions and noticed in them substantial number and variety. The information was culled mainly from inscriptions published in *Epigraphia Indica*, *Corpus Inscriptionum Indicarum*, etc., besides some journals and gradually this monograph took shape. However, when it was ready and was to be given to the publisher, Dr Sarkar and I felt that it required restructuring; in fact, we had started rewriting the chapters. For one reason or the other, this could not be completed as planned and the work was, as is usually said, "lost in the mists of time", since all this happened more than twenty-five years ago sometime in 1971-72 or 1972-73. The work in fact exemplifies the adage "better is the enemy of good" as I have been telling my friends.

Dr Haribishnu Sarkar was my senior colleague and mentor and I had the highest regard for his scholarship and other qualities. His unfortunate demise totally forestalled the possibility of rewriting the book. On being goaded by my friends and family members and having obtained the consent of Smt Manjusri Sarkar, I decided to publish the monograph in its original form. This, I found, was no easy task either.

The manuscript as well as the drawings and other material had to be ferretted out from piles of my several half- or unwritten research papers and sundry writings and notes. To my dismay, the text-figures which had been so painstakingly prepared and pasted had got mixed up because of the time gap. Thanks to the help volunteered by Shri C. Dorje, my former colleague in the Archaeological Survey of India, these could be retrieved and were than assiduously retraced by Shri M.S. Mani who also finalized them for publication. Incidentally, Shri Mani had prepared the original tracings and arranged the text-figures when we were working on this monograph more than twenty-five years ago.

This work cannot claim to be an exhaustive study of *all* symbols and graphic representations in inscriptions and we were fully conscious of this when we prepared this monograph; we had also noticed that several examples had been either omitted or missed. It also does not include symbols, etc., occurring in Arabic and Persian inscriptions as well as in ancient Indian seals; the latter have been exhaustively studied by K.K. Thaplyal in his *Studies in Ancient Indian Seals* (1972). We have also not included symbols in coins and sculptural representations which have respectively been discussed by Savita Sharma in her exhaustive work *Early Indian Symbols: Numismatic Evidence* (1990) and Rai Govind Chandra in his *Indian Symbolism: Symbols as Sources of our Customs and Beliefs* (1996). In our work we have, of course, included a chart with the symbols and graphic representations in inscriptions and their parallels in early Indian coins, graffiti in pottery, signs in Harappan seals, masons' marks and tattoo marks, both ancient and modern, etc. While this is essentially a study of symbols and graphic representations in Indian inscriptions, a few examples have also been included from inscriptions found in Afghanistan, Nepal, Sri Lanka, Java and of course Pakistan and Bangladesh. Since this monograph is being published almost in its original form as written more than twenty-five years ago, we have not included the examples published in post-1973 *Epigraphia Indica*, *Corpus Inscriptionum Indicarum* and other later publications, which would have certainly added to the value of this monograph. The only change that we have made is in the name of certain states like Karnataka in place of Mysore, Tamil Nadu in place of Madras, etc. It has not been possible for us to follow the changes in districts which in recent years have been subjected to all kinds of changes by way of renaming or division.

Discerning readers will find several shortcomings in this work about which we were quite conscious: I am sure that further and more detailed studies will be taken up in future taking into account the entire corpus of information.

I would like to express my gratitude towards the staff members of the Central Archaeological Library of the Archaeological Survey of India, and

Smt Poornima Ray, in-charge of the library of the Delhi Circle of the Archaeological Survey of India for their cooperation and help. Shri M.S. Mani deserves all praise for his ready help in resurrecting all over again the drawings which he had originally prepared for us more than twenty-five years ago. My friend and highly talented graphic designer Shri Ranmal Singh Jhala has designed the cover in his usual imaginative manner even though I could not make available to him all the required illustrative material in the form of photographs. To Dr Arundhati Banerji, Deputy Superintending Archaeologist in the Archaeological Survey of India and Shri Sovan Chatterjee, I owe a debt of gratitude for photographs of inscriptions; these have been included mainly as illustrative examples and to convey to the reader the idea about the symbols and graphic representations in relation to the inscription. Dr Banerji in fact prepared for me the list of inscriptions which are included here as plates. Shri R.S. Bisht, Director in the Archaeological Survey of India provided me the necessary help and support for which I am beholden to him. Copyright of the photographs rests with the Archaeological Survey of India.

My friend Dr José Pereira read the original typescript and made several suggestions which were incorporated by us.

All praise for Shri Vikas Arya of Aryan Books International for not only bringing out this publication so nicely but also for his patience; any one else would have abandoned it for the inordinate delay on my part throughout the various stages of publication of the monograph.

Finally, I would like to thank my family members; my son Siddhartha in particular helped me in the onerous task of preparing the index.

New Delhi **B.M. Pande**
1st January 1999

CONTENTS

LIST OF FIGURES

11. Floral designs: 1 Basim plates of Vākāṭaka Vindhyaśakti II, AD 400; 2 grants of Pravarasena II of Vākāṭaka family; 3 Andhavaram plates of Anantaśakti-varman, fifth century; 4 Kabul inscription of Shāhī Khiṅgala, sixth-seventh century; 5 Talegaon copper plates of Krishṇa-Rāja I, AD 768; 6 Rāshṭrakūṭa record from Cambay, of Govinda IV, AD 930; 7 Chidivalasa plates of Devendravarman, AD 893-895; 8 Masulipatam plates of Chālukya-Bhīma II, AD 934-945; 9 Chebrolu inscription of Jaya; 10 Pillalamarri inscription of the reign of Kāpaya Nāyaka, Śaka 1279; 11 Patnapada grant of Choḍa Bhaktirāja, Śaka 1265; 12 Patna Museum plates of Raṇabhañja; 13 Kendupatna plates of Narasiṁha II, AD 1294; 14 Madras Museum plates of the time of Narendradhavala, tenth century; 15 Ramesvaram inscription of Niśśaṅkamalla, AD 1187; 16 Bodh-Gaya inscription of the time of Sena kings of Bengal
12. Floral, ornamental or vegetal symbols: 1 Howraghat plates of Balavarman III of Kāmarūpa, AD 829; 2 Parbatiya plates of Vanamālavarmadeva; 3 Hulgur inscription of Khoṭṭiga, a Rāshṭrakūṭa ruler, AD 972; 4 Asoge plates of Kadamba Jayakeśin (II), AD 1134; 5 Balera plates of Mūlarāja I of the Anahilvad branch of the Chālukyas, AD 995; 6 inscription of Kadamba Tribhuvanamalla, AD 1107; 7 records from Raipur, twelfth century; 8 Pallava record of Kumāravishṇu II; 9 Hottur (Dharwar) inscription of the reign of Someśvara I, AD 1067; 10 Vandram and Maliyapundi grants of Ammarāja II; 11 Ranastipundi grant of Vimalāditya; 12 Teki plates of Rājarāja Choḍagaṅga, AD 1084; 13 Masulipatam plates of Amma II, Eastern Chālukya, AD 945-70; 14 Akkalapundi grants of Siṅgaya Nāyaka, Śaka-Saṁvat 1300; 15 Vanapalli plates of Anna-Vema Śaka-Saṁvat 1300; 16 Donepundi grants of Nāmaya-Nāyaka, Śaka-Saṁvat 1259; 17 Gadivore grant of Shashṭhadeva II, AD 1262; 18 Dhar *praśasti* of Arjunavarman, thirteenth century AD; 19 *praśasti* in the temple of Lakhamandal at Madha in Jaunsar Bawar, about seventh-eighth century AD; 20 Chhoti Sadri stone inscription; 21 Prince of Museum plates of Dadda III, a Gurjara chief; 22 inscription from Chitaldurg district
13. Wheel or *chakra*: 1 Mathura stone image inscription of Kumāragupta I, AD 454-55; 2 Nachne-ki-Talai inscription of Mahārāja Prithvisheṇa, Vākāṭaka ruler; 3 Vākāṭaka inscription from Ganj; 4 Jodhpur inscription of Pratihāra Bāuka, Vikrama-Saṁvat 894 (AD 837); 5 Torkhede copper-plate grant of the time of Govindarāja, Śaka-Saṁvat 735 (AD 812); 6 Pilgrim's record in a Kākatiya inscription from Gaya, twelfth-thirteenth century; 7 Krishnapuram plate of the Vijayanagara king Sadāśivarāya, Śaka-Saṁvat 1489; 8 inscription of Jishṇugupta, from Nepal

14. *Śaṅkha* or conch-shell: 1 grant of Prithivīchandra Bhogaśakti, Kalachuri ruler, from Anjaneri, AD 709-10; 2 Pabhosa inscription, circa seventh-eighth century AD; 3 Chidivalasa plates of Devendravarman, Gaṅga year 397, ninth century; 4 Western Chālukya record from Kurgod, Bellary, twelfth century; 5 Jodhpur inscription of Pratihāra Bāuka, AD 837; 6 Kottayam plate of Vīra Rāghava, circa fourteenth century AD; 7 Lucknow Museum plate of Kīrtipāla, AD 1111; 8 copper plate grant from Balasore, Orissa; 9 Baudh grant of Raṇabhañjadeva, 54th year of Bhañja dynasty; 10 inscription of the time of Kākatīya Pratāparudra I from Gaya, thirteenth century; 11 Kolur inscription of the reign of Yādava Siṅghana, thirteenth century

15. 1 Chhoti Sadri stone inscription, fifth century AD; 2 Pali copper plate grant of Mahārāja Lakshmaṇa, Saṁvat 158, fifth-sixth century; 3 Srirangam plates of Vīra-Harihara-Rāya-Udaiyar (III), Śaka 1336; 4 Bandh plates of Salonabhañja, fourteenth century; 5 Kharepatan plates of Raṭṭarāja, AD 1008-9; 6 Bichapalli western Chālukyan inscription of Bhuvanaikamalla's time, AD 1074; 7 Rāshṭrakūṭa grant from Chinchani, Śaka 848 (AD 926); 8 Begur inscription of Eṟeyappa, AD 908 and 938; 9 Jain rock-inscriptions at Vallimalai, Śaka-Saṁvat 899; 10 Khanapur plates of Mādhavavarman, seventh century AD; 11 plates of Dantivarman of Gujarat, Śaka Saṁvat 789; 12 Prince of Wales Museum plates of Govindarāja, AD 810; 13 copper-plate of Dhruva II of the Gujarat Rāshṭrakūṭa branch, AD 884; 14 Akkalkot inscription of Śilāhāra Indarasa, western Chālukya, AD 1114; 15 Jodhpur plates of the time of Durlabhharāja, Vikrama-Saṁvat 1069 (AD 1013); 16 Velur rock-inscription of Nolamba king Kannaradeva, AD 940-956; 17 Orissa plates of Vidyādharabhañja-deva, circa twelfth-thirteenth century; 18 Kamauli plate of Govindachandra, (Vikrama) Saṁvat 1182 (AD 1126); 19 Banskhera plate of Harsha, early seventh century; 20 Balera plates of Mūlarāja I, AD 995; 21 Chiruvroli grant of Hambīra, Śaka 1383; 22 grant of Raghudeva, Śaka 1378; 23 Kanker plates of Pamparājadeva, AD 1213-14; 24 Saheth-Maheth plate of Govindachandra, AD 1128-29; 25 Mehar plate of Dāmodaradeva, AD 1234

16. Gajatame, Aśokan rock-edict, Kalsi, third century BC

17. Fish: 1 Nepalese inscription; 2 and 3 copper-plate grants of Saindhavas of Bhūtāmbilikā, Gujarat; 4 and 5 Ranganatha inscription of Sundara Pāṇḍya, AD 1250-51

18. Birds and mythical figures: 1 Akkalapundi grant of Siṅgaya Nāyaka, District Godavari, Andhra Pradesh, AD 1368; 2 Dantewara Sanskrit and Hindi inscriptions of Dikpāladeva, from Jagdalpur, Madhya

Pradesh, AD 1702; 3 Pentapadu grant of Choḍa Bhaktirāja, Śaka 1265; 4 Saheth-Maheth plate of Govindachandra, AD 1128-29; 5 Ajayagadh stone inscription of Nana, Vikrama Saṁvat 1345

19. Religious edifices: 1 sacrificial altar, inscription from Sonda, AD 1674; 2 inscription in Gaṇeśa Ratha, Mahabalipuram, seventh century

20. 1 Mahudi plates of Paramāra Bhoja, Vikrama Saṁvat 1074 (AD 1018); 2 Harsola copper plate grant of (Paramāra) Sīyaka, Vikrama Saṁvat 1005 (AD 949); 3 Grant of Sīyaka, Vikrama Saṁvat 1026 (AD 968); 4 Record of Vākpati-Muñja, Vikrama Saṁvat 1038 (AD 981); 5 Mandhata plates of Jayasiṁhadeva of Dhāra, (Vikrama) Saṁvat 1112 (AD 1055-56); 6 Banswara plates of Bhojadeva (Vikrama) Saṁvat 1076 (AD 1020); 7 Bhopal plates of Mahādeva (Vikrama) Saṁvat 1076 (AD 1020); 8 Mehar plate of Dāmodaradeva, Vikrama Saṁvat 1156 (AD 1234); 9 Kadambapadraka grant of Naravarman, AD 1159; 10 Mandhata plates of Devapāla; 11 Mandhata plates of Paramāra Jayasiṁha-Jayavarma, AD 1274

21. Boar incarnation of Vishṇu: 1 copper plate grant from Bihar, AD 1026; 2 Lucknow Museum plate of Kīrtipāla AD 1111; 3 grant of Prithivīchandra Bhogaśakti from Anjaneri, eighth century

22. 1 Garra plates of Chandella Trailokyavarman, AD 1205; 2 Chandella records of Madanavarmadeva; 3 Pachar plate of Paramardideva, AD 1171; 4 Charkhari plates of Hammīradeva, AD 1171; 4 Mahoba plates of Paramardideva, AD 1289

23. 1 Shakardarra Kharoshṭhī inscription of the year 40 (second-first century); 2 inscription of Kampana from Taṭākapurīśvara temple at Madan, AD 1362-63; 3 Gaya inscription mentioning Govindapāla, AD 1175; 4 Someśvara temple, Mindigul inscription of Rājādhirāja, Śaka Saṁvat 970 (AD 1047-48); 5 Narayanpal inscription of Guṇḍa Mahādevi, Śaka 1033 (AD 1111); 6 Bitragunta grant of Saṅgama II, early thirteenth century; 7 Jambukeśvaram grant of Vijayaranga Chokkanātha Nāyaka, Śaka 1630; 8 Pushpagiri inscription of the time of Yādava Singhana, early thirteenth century; 9 Machupalle inscription of the time of Somideva-Mahārāja, Śaka 1178 (AD 1255); 10 Anmakonda pillar inscription of Prola, AD 1117

24. Imprecatory scenes: 1 Rājapura copper plates of Madhurāntakadeva, Śaka 987; 2 Bodh-Gaya inscription of the time of Aśokachalla-Lakshmaṇa, Saṁvat 74 (AD 1194)

25. Graphic representations: 1 Tirath rock-inscription, Swat Valley; 2 Ci-Aruton inscription, Java; 3 Duwe Gala cave inscription, Sri Lanka

26. Nepal, lotus drawn in an inscription

LIST OF PLATES

CHAPTER 1

INTRODUCTION

Symbols cannot be said to be just meaningless marks scratched at one's whim; nor are they simple conventional signs or representations of some apparent object, idea or process. Each of them has a deeper meaning, sometimes even invested with certain magico-religious properties; each of them have "specific connotations in addition to its conventional and obvious meaning".[1] Once read in correct perspective they reveal their hidden world—and lost language. As a matter of fact, myths, legends, magical rites, religious ceremonies, cosmological speculations of early societies have often been expressed through some symbol or the other.

Many of these symbols might have originated in the dark recesses of the unconscious, although in course of time they acquired an accepted meaning and recognised value. Recent researches in psychoanalysis, ethnology and the history of religion have greatly widened the scope of the study of symbols and symbolism. Symbolic thinking is considered as 'an autonomous mode of cognition'. 'It is consubstantial with human existence, it comes before language and discursive reason'.[2]

The cryptic forms of symbols, abstract drawings of primitive or children's art are manifestations of this aspect of the human psyche. Modern painting and sculpture might have perhaps had their roots also in this deep abyss of the unconscious.

But never can any symbol have any immutable meaning or form, as symbolic thinking always finds its 'new mask'.

It changes with the times, with the people living in variable geographical, social, cultural and psychological types of environment. Sometimes even the meaning may be modified with the creation of new ideas and philosophies. Its geographical horizon is also not constant for it migrates from place to place and from one culture to another.

In the symbolic presentation of an object or a figure there is a definite abandonment of details and a violent departure from reality. Only a few traits are emphasized to convey the obvious and immediate meaning of a figure. Eventually, it is transformed into a conventional sign or stylized form. A pair of horns may represent a bull or a ram, a spiral, an elephant's trunk or a conch-shell and so on. In popular usage, a symbol is generally conceived as the one with such abstract, conventional form. Evidently, it is far removed from the realm of naturalistic art. In this respect symbols have family-likeness with the children's or primitive art. But as will be shown presently, not all symbols belong to this category. What is called formal symbolism has no bearing with "objects of experience or phenomena of nature, but which are entirely absolute, just as the letter X is absolute and arbitrary".[3] Thus a circle may represent an ideal of perfection or completion, a spiral the latent vital force of the universe or the human psyche.

But a symbol need not necessarily be a conventionalized picture. Even a naturalistic form may serve as a vehicle of symbolic expression. Take for instance, the elephant in the Aśokan edict at Kalsi. It certainly falls in the domain of graphic art; the elephant is drawn realistically and its every curve reverberates with dynamic rhythm. Yet it is a symbol—with an inner meaning. It symbolizes Buddha—the white elephant that entered in a dream into the womb of his mother. A symbol, then may be a graphic representation or a conventionalized drawing or a pictographic representation.

In many cases symbols originally represented natural objects like hills, plants, animals, rivers and several other phenomena. All these representations might be having a pictographic effect, may be with some mythic or cosmological background. Some of the symbols followed the geometric pattern, incidentally representing certain naturalistic feature of the plant and animal kingdoms, and the inanimate world around. But the imitation of natural phenomena was not motivated by any sense of beauty. The engravings of the Lower Aurignacian phase are either "simple spirals and frets or crude representations of animals' and 'were intended to fulfil a magical function".[4] Several symbols might have come into existence as a result of magical rites—as a result of practising sympathetic magic. Many of the animal symbolism in religion and art also sprang from the primitive concept of totem animal symbolizing "each tribesman's identity with the tribal unit".[5] In a nutshell, the totemic concept is also a psychological experience expressed through oral as well as visual forms.

Some scholars in recent times have shown the dependence of visual art to the other art-forms like mythology, drama, folklore, etc. "Even when this art veers towards abstraction, as in decorative design, it often gives evidence of descent from some image or episode mentioned in folk-tale, proverb, song or other orally transmitted tradition".[6] Thus, mythology and other types of oral art play a great role in determining the form and content of the primitive art and also of symbol. Mircea Eliade in his *Images and Symbols* has shown how oral forms of art often determine the form and meaning of a symbol. He writes in a different context: "One should strive to grasp the symbolic meaning of the religious facts in their heterogeneous, yet structurally interlocking appearances; such facts can be rites of ritual behaviour as well as myths or legends or supernatural beings".[7] He also admits the dependence of symbols upon some precise historical situation. For instance, "It is evident that the horse could not have become among other things a symbol of death before being domesticated."

Harold Bayley has shown that the Christian symbols have a long esoteric tradition and are associated with divine myth and sacraments. In fact "symbolism is the language of Christian and every other form of symbolism".[8] As there has been an unbroken tradition, the meanings of these Christian symbols are fairly well-known, while those belonging to several other religions lost their latent significance. Who knows that the hidden meanings of these are not unknown to those few initiated ones in India, more so, the Tantriks. Again, the meaning of the symbols may not appear mysterious once the probable myths, legends and lore connected with them are exploited and their relationship established.

Indian mythology, art and religion have boundless profusion of animal symbolism. Every god or goddess has his or her animal vehicle. Sometimes an animal stands for the theriomorphic representation of a god. The bull is not only a vehicle of Śiva but also his theriomorphic representation. All this symbolism in Indian religions may have been derived from primitive practices. Likewise, several other symbols like tree or tree-within-railing, hill, standard or *dhvaja*, etc., entered into developed cultural group from the primitive. The worship of the tree or tree-within-railing is a very ancient custom and on the basis of inscriptional and sculptural evidence the symbol, also appearing as a favourite coin-device, may easily be identified as *chaityas*.[9] It was adopted by the Buddhists too, and in Bharhut reliefs all the past Buddhas are represented by their trees.[10] All this may show how deep-rooted are these trends—the trends of primitive symbolism born out of myths, legends, folkore, etc.

The influence of primitive symbolism is manifest not only in Indian art and religion but also in several other spheres, where, however, the conventional forms have a dominant role to play. Such symbols occur as part of the writing on the Harappan seals and sealings,[11] as graffiti on protohistoric and megalithic pottery,[12] as symbols on ancient Indian coins,[13] as auspicious symbols in inscriptions and manuscripts, as Tantrik hieroglyphics,[14] and also as tattoo marks[15] and masons' marks.[16] There are several other sources of Indian symbolism like the floor-decoration by means of dried or wet rice-powder, murals on rural or aboriginal huts, rock-paintings, etc.[17] Even the paintings on pottery may include symbols in conventionalized or naturalistic forms. Harold Bayley has shown how water-marks into paper and printer's marks 'constitute a coherent and unbroken chain of *emblems*' of primitive Christianity as well as other forms of mysticism. "Most of these signs have entirely lost their primitive significance, and are now used purely for commercial purposes; but there was a time when they were not only trade signs, but were also hieroglyphics, under which the pearl of great price was revered".[18]

Of all the sources, symbols on coins and graffiti marks on pottery have been studied extensively although it has not been possible to decipher satisfactorily their meanings. Some studies of a restricted nature are available on mason's marks and tattoo-designs[19] but no exclusive study on the symbols appearing in Indian inscriptions has yet been undertaken. However, it was G. Bühler who had already made a beginning of this study in his book, *Indian Palaeography*.[20] He writes: "In accordance with the ancient Brahmanical maxim, which requires a Maṅgala, a benediction or an auspicious word at the beginning, in the middle and at the end of a composition in order to ensure its completion and preservation, sacred symbols of auspicious import are found at the beginning and the end of two edicts, and of many inscriptions of the next four centuries" It is, however, not correct when he says that "the most common Maṅgala-symbols, employed in this way are the well-known *Svastika*, the trident or the so-called *Triratna* symbol resting on the *Dharmacakra*, and the conventional representation of a *Caitya* tree".[21] According to the present authors, the most oft-repeated symbol is the one supposedly employed for *Oṁ* or *Siddhaṁ*. In fact, Ojha,[22] Dani[23] and D.C. Sircar[24] have already indicated it in their studies. Dani has even tried to show the development of this symbol but his findings are based on random sampling rather than on systematic collection of data. Conclusions drawn in the present study on this symbol are, therefore, quite different from those of Dani.

All the publications mentioned above are practically without any illustrations, and further, no attempt has been made therein to show the distribution and development of these symbols and their parallels in other types of Indian symbolism. In the following pages an attempt is made to study the different aspects of symbols occurring in Indian epigraphs. For the purpose of the present study, sculptural ornamentation, other than the imprecatory scenes above the inscriptions, and the symbols or emblems on the seals attached to the copper-plates, have not been taken into account despite the fact that it is not always possible to draw a clear line of differentiation between sculptures and reliefs conveying *maṅgala* idea and those without any auspicious import. The representations on memorial pillars, *sati*-stones and sculptures etc., are therefore, excluded from the purview of the present study.

Symbols occurring in Indian inscriptions may have conventionalized or naturalistic forms. Besides these two groups, there are representations of gods and goddesses, and imprecatory scenes in the inscriptions. The last category constitutes a class of its own and it is doubtful whether these images belong to the realm of symbols. Yet they cannot be excluded from the scope of the present study for these representations form a phase in the use of symbolism in inscriptions. Their use conveys a meaning and significance. Gradually they replaced the symbols but the idea behind both might have remained unchanged. Perhaps it is a case of changing of the guise — or to use Mircea Eliade's expression, 'mask'.

Notes and References

1. Carl G. Jung, *Man and His Symbols* (London, 1964), p. 20.
2. Mircea Eliade, *Images and Symbols* (London, 1961), pp. 9-12. He writes elsewhere: "Finally, a considerable role in the vogue for symbolism must be attributed to the researches of certain philosophers, epistemologists, and linguists who wanted to show the symbolic character not only of language, but also of all other activities of the human spirit, from rite and myth to art and science. Since man has a 'symbol-forming power,' all that he produces is symbolic". See his 'Methodological remarks on the study of religious symbolism' in *The History of Religions*, edited by Mircea Eliade and Joseph M. Kitagawa (Chicago, 1959), p. 87. Symbols are also considered as a useful collection of source material for the psychological patterns of ancient people. See Beatrice Laura Goff, *Symbols of Prehistoric Mesopotamia* (New Haven and London, 1963), p. xxxiii.
3. Herbert Read, *The Meaning of Art* (Pelican, 1950), p. 168.
4. Leonhard Adam, *Primitive Art* (London, 1963), pp. 81-84.
5. Carl G. Jung, *op.cit.*, pp. 238-39. Also, Sigmund Freud, *Totem and Taboo* (New York, 1946).
6. Douglas Fraser, *The Many Faces of Primitive Art* (New Jersey, 1966), p. 264.
7. Mircea Eliade (1959), *op. cit.*, p. 97.
8. Harold Bayley, *The Lost Language of Symbolism* (London, 1912), Vol. II, p. 350.
9. A. Ghosh and H. Sarkar, 'Beginnings of sculptural art in south-east India: a stele from Amaravati', *Ancient India*, nos. 20 & 21 (1967), p. 171. Also,

H. Sarkar, *Studies in Early Buddhist Architecture of India* (Delhi, 1966), pp. 4-5.

10. Alexander Cunningham, *The Stupa of Bharhut* (London, 1879), pp. 45-47.
11. Sir John Marshall, *Mohenjo-daro and the Indus Civilization* (London, 1931), Vol. II, pp. 370-422; Earnest J.H. Mackay, *Further Excavations at Mohenjo-daro* (Delhi, 1940), Vol. I, pp. 316-356; G.R. Hunter, *The Script of Harappa and Mohenjo-daro and its Connection with other Scripts* (London, 1934); Alan S.C. Ross, *The 'Numeral Signs' of the Mohenjo-daro Script,* Memoirs of the Archaeological Survey of India, no. 57 (Delhi, 1938).
12. B.B. Lal, 'From the Megalithic to the Harappa; tracing back the graffiti on the pottery,' *Ancient India*, no. 16 (1960), pp. 4-24.
13. John Allan, *Catalogue of the Coins of ancient India in the British Museum* (London, 1936).
14. While propounding his theory of the origin of the Devanāgarī alphabet from Tāntrik hieroglyphs, Shamasastry has described several Tāntrik symbols mentioned in different Tāntrik texts. See, *Indian Antiquary*, XXXV (1906). Swami Sankarananda has also made an attempt to decipher Indus script by means of Tāntrik hieroglyphs. See his *The Dictionary of Indian Hieroglyphs* (Calcutta, 1963).
15. B. A. Gupte, 'Notes on female tattoo-designs in India', *Indian Antiquary*, XXXI (1902), pp. 293-98; H. A. Rose, 'Notes on female tattooing in the Panjab,' *ibid.*, p. 297; C.E. Luard, 'Tattooing in Central India,' *ibid.*, XXXIII (1904), pp. 219-228, 237-249, 280-289 and 301-309; and B.A. Gupte, 'Notes on female tattooing from Ootacamund,' *ibid.*, XXXV (1906), pp. 269-270. There are chapters on tattooing in several monographs devoted to the aboriginal tribes in India.
16. M.J. Walhouse, 'Mason's Marks,' *Indian Antiquary*, IV (1875), pp. 302-305; H. Rivett-Carnac, 'Mason's marks from old buildings in the North-west Provinces of India', *ibid.*, VII (1878), pp. 295-298; A. Gorham, *Mason's Marks of the Mughal Dynasty* (London, 1911) dealing primarily with the marks appearing on the Indo-Islamic monuments. Also, H. Sarkar, 'Chronological aspects of Mason's Marks from Nagarjunakonda', *Bharati*, Nos. 12-14 (Varanasi, 1968-71), pp. 226-235.
17. 'With them can be associated, as belonging to the same kind of hieroglyphic art, the banner of cognizances of gods and heroes mentioned in the Epics, those still used by Paṇḍās at *tīrthas* to facilitate recognition by visiting pilgrims, tattoo marks ancient and modern, cattle-brands, and folk art generally.' See Ananda K. Coomaraswamy, *History of Indian and Indonesian Art* (London, 1927), p. 44.
18. Harold Bayley, *op.cit.*, I, p. 3
19. Cunningham (*op.cit.*, pp. 39-40, pl. LII) has discussed the practice of tattooing amongst the aboriginal tribes of India. He has also shown the practice of tattooing on all the female sculptures in Bharhut and the repertory of designs includes: sun, moon, several small flowers, star, bird or *triśūla*. The tattoo

marks in Bharhut sculptures occur on the cheek-bones, chin and breast. Cunningham has envisaged that the practice of tattooing amongst the modern tribals of the area (Kols) must be following the ancient methods as in vogue during Aśoka's time.

20. G. Bühler, *Indian Palaeography* (reprinted Calcutta, 1959), p. 109.
21. *Ibid.*, p. 109.
22. Gaurishankar Hirachand Ojha, *Bhāratīya Prāchīna Lipimālā* (in Hindi), (Ajmer V.S. 1975), pp. 148-49; also utilized by Sarabhai Manilal Nawab, *Jaina Chitrakalpadruma* (in Gujarati), (Ahmedabad, 1936), pp. 57-61.
23. A.H. Dani, *Indian Palaeography* (Oxford, 1963), pp. 121, 122.
24. D.C. Sircar, *Indian Epigraphy* (Delhi, 1965).

CHAPTER 2

EARLY SYMBOLS

The majority of the symbols appearing in early Indian inscriptions fall in the period from the third century BC to about the third century AD. Compared to this vast span of time, the number of symbols noticed so far do not by any means constitute a rich repository. Moreover, the practice of inscribing auspicious marks in inscriptions never came in wide vogue in any period of Indian history. As a result, it is difficult to follow the course of development of individual symbols for any length of time. In many cases, the practice remained confined to a particular region in a particular period.

Chronologically, early symbols clearly show two periods of their emergence, viz., (a) symbols belonging to third century BC and (b) those appearing in the records of the period between the first century BC and the second-third centuries AD. The second phase seems to be relatively richer in symbols than the first. In the first phase are included the inscriptions of Aśoka (fig. 1, *1*), the Sohagaura copper-plate (fig. 1, *2*) and the Rampurva copper bolt containing four marks made of lines of impressed dots[1] (fig. 1, *3*), all datable to the third century BC. The Sohagaura plate contains the largest number of seven symbols or representations, interpretation of which varies from scholar to scholar (*EI*, XXII, p. 1).[2]

So far only three inscriptions of Aśoka are known to have yielded symbols which are of three different kinds, viz., (i) ogee variety of *svastika*, (ii) taurine symbol, and (iii) triskelion (fig. 1, *1*). The *svastika* and the taurine symbols occur in the Jaugada version of the two separate rock-edicts (pl. III), while triskelion is found at the opening of the Erragudi and the Rajula-Mandagiri minor rock-edicts (*EI*, XXXI, p. 211 and XXXII, p. 1). These symbols may, therefore, be taken as belonging to the earliest group so far as their occurrence in inscriptions is concerned. It is worth noting that the three symbols of the Aśokan edicts provide a link with the different series of early coins. But the three symbols on the Aśokan inscriptions occur rather

Fig. 1. Early symbols: 1 *svastika* and taurine symbols from Aśokan rock-edict at Jaugada, triskelion from minor rock-edicts of Aśoka at Erragudi and Rajula-Mandagiri; 2 copper plate from Sohagaura; 3 Rampurva copper bolt; 4 Kailvan

infrequently on the silver punch-marked coins.[3] Further the ogee variety of *svastika* appears for the first time on the issues collectively known as tribal coins.

Of the seven symbols (fig. 1, *2*) appearing on the Sohagaura copper plate, the hill surmounted by a crescent is a very popular motif on ancient Indian coins. Other devices like tree-within-railing, representation of structures etc., bear little resemblance with those on the ancient Indian coins. In fact some of the representations on the Sohagaura plate do not look like symbols. Two structures, generally identified as granaries, and one of the trees have more or less naturalistic appearance; the hill surmounted by a crescent, a spoon-like object, a U-shaped mark, etc., however constitute conventionalized forms on the Sohagaura inscription. These symbols arranged in a row above the text are said to have some bearing with the contents of the inscription: "The two trees probably signify the drought stage from leaf-some to leafless, and the houses for stores." Some authorities (*EI*, XXII, p. 1) take the hill surmounted by moon combined with the next symbol as the monogrammatic representation of the name Chandragupta, the famous Maurya king. These scholars date the inscription to pre-Aśokan times. The general consensus, however, is to place it later than Aśoka.

The four symbols made of lines of impressed dots, in the Rampurva copper bolt, include the hill-with-crescent, the taurine or *Nandipāda*, the open cross and vertical eye with a dot in the centre.[4]

Symbols represented on the Aśokan edicts and the Sohagaura plate are absent in the next period when new marks seem to have been introduced. Several of them are without any parallel in the different series of symbols on ancient Indian coins. In this period different forms of triangles, three-armed or three-pronged symbols became popular. A striking feature is their concentration in western India, and to a certain extent, on the east coast including Orissa. In other words, such symbols are common in the cave-inscriptions belonging mostly to the Buddhist settlements. Their occurrence in the Jaina establishments of Mathura and Orissa is also interesting.

The cave inscriptions from western India alone have yielded no less than sixty symbols conforming broadly to ten different types. Next in order comes Orissa where only three varieties are noticed. In the rest of India symbols appear only sporadically in the inscriptions. Mention may be made here of the occurrence of four or five symbols in a Brāhmī inscription from Kailvan (fig. 1, *4*), district Patna, datable to AD 186 (*EI*, XXXI, p. 229). These were inscribed in a sequence: a narrow-necked vase, a double-pronged standard, two *svastikas* one above the other, the lower one dovetailed with the preceding symbol and forming a *ḍamaru*-shaped symbol. This is also the period when *svastika* and *triratna* attained height of their popularity

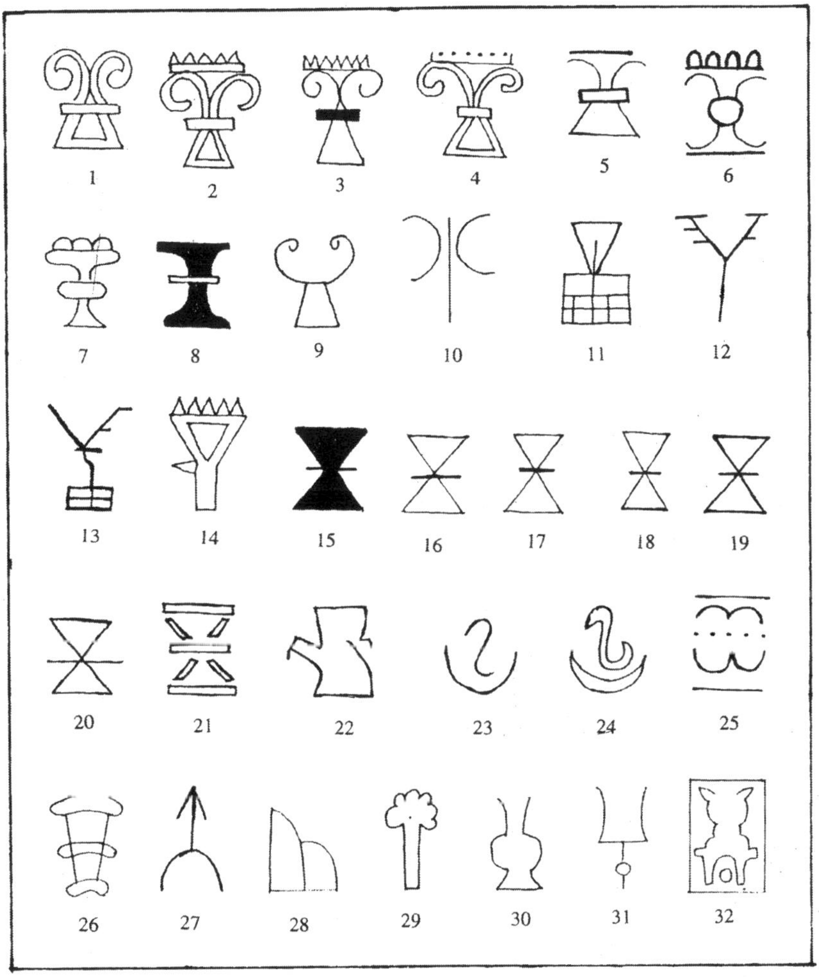

Fig. 2. Early symbols: 1-3 Kuda; 4 Mahad; 5-7 Junnar; 8-9 Kuda; 10 Kol; 11 Hathigumpha; 12 Manchapuri; 13 Bagh; 14 Gunji; 15-17 Kuda; 18-19 Nasik; 20 Karle; 21 Kuda; 22 Kailvan; 23 Bhaja; 24 Karle; 25 Kuda; 26 Nasik; 27 Barnala; 28 Gunji; 29 Jankhat; 30-31 Kailvan; 32 Kuda

in different parts of India. It has also to be borne in mind that the auspicious symbol which was later used as the opening formula of the inscriptions started being used only in this period; the symbol first occurring in some Kushāṇa records has been read variously as *siddhaṁ* or *Oṁ*. The history of this symbol, which outlived all other types, is stretched over a period of a millennium-and-a-half; the evolution of this auspicious mark is discussed separately in Chapter 4.

How the use of symbols in inscriptions assumed such proportions in the west coast is difficult to ascertain. Of all the sites, Kuda seems to be the richest in symbols accounting for seven different types. But in frequency Junnar comes first, with twenty-two examples conforming to only three broad varieties; Kuda has yielded about sixteen specimens.[5] Yet new forms are not confined to these two places alone, for some varieties found at Bhaja, Karle and Nasik have no analogy amongst the known symbols appearing on early Indian coins. On the other hand, those occurring in the inscriptions from Hathigumpha, Manchapuri and Bagh caves in Orissa bear broad similarity with symbols on coins. Evidently, western India received some symbols from certain extraneous source; once the symbols are analyzed individually, this fact becomes clearly evident.

Generally, cave inscriptions from western India commence with a symbol like *svastika, triratna, ḍamaru* etc., but there are several instances of symbols used at the opening as well as at the end of an inscription. Sometimes *svastikas* have been used at both the places. In an inscription from Junnar (fig. 2, *6, 7*) *triratna* has been engraved at the beginning of both the lines of the inscription while two other symbols occur respectively at the end of lines 1 and 2. At Mahad (fig. 2, *4*) symbols are placed side by side above the inscription. Yet another interesting variation comes from Kuda (fig. 2, *1-3, 15-17*) where two symbols are incised at the end of the last line, a *ḍamaru* symbol appearing at the opening.[6] The Hathigumpha inscription of Khāravela (fig. 2, *11*) ends with a triangular standard-within-railing while a three-pronged symbol and a *svastika* are found on the top left margin of the inscription.[7]

As already stated, many of the symbols are not known from other sources; as a result, it is not easy to evolve a commonly-acceptable nomenclature. Further, those already known have, in some cases, more than one name for the same symbol. For example, three-pronged symbols have been termed variously as *triratna, nandipāda, triśūla* etc., but the correctness of the name depends on the context in which the symbol is put to use. Sometimes it becomes different to describe the symbol, not to speak of giving a name, for, in symbolism rejection or distortion of natural forms is accompanied by definite abandonment of details in preference to one or two elements in an object. All this makes the classification of early symbols a hazardous task. What is attempted here is a broad classification based either on already-known types or, in case of new ones, on the superficial appearance.

Broadly speaking, symbols occurring in early inscriptions may be divided into five groups, viz., (A) taurine and double-limbed symbols, (B) triskelion and *triratna*, (C) triangles, (D) *svastikas*, and (E) the miscellaneous symbols; each group may further be sub-divided. Each group will now be dealt with separately; the *svastika* is dealt with in the next chapter (Chapter 3).

A. Taurine and double-limbed symbols

Four different symbols are included in this group, viz., (i) taurine symbol, (ii) one looking like ram's head, (iii) two-limbed symbol, and (iv) two-pronged symbol.

(i) *Taurine symbol*: The earliest example of taurine symbol comes from the Jaugada versions of the two separate rock-edicts of Aśoka (fig. 1, *1*; pl. III). At the top of the separate rock-edict II are found two ogee *svastikas*, whereas three taurine symbols and a *svastika* occupy the place in between edicts II and I, these marks, as it were, serving as the dividing line. These taurine symbols have been identified by scholars like Hultzsch as the Brāhmī letter *ma*[8] (below, p. 25).

The Nasik cave inscription of the time of Kṛishṇa ends with a taurus symbol preceded by a *svastika*. The inscription is dated to the second half of the first century BC (*EI*, VIII, p. 93). Particularly interesting is an early short inscription from Sanchi (*EI*, II, p. 480) reading *si ha ya* which is preceded by a *svastika* and ends with Brahmi *ma* or a taurus symbol; in addition, there is a symbol respectively above and below this inscription (pl. IA). These symbols proved to be a favourite device on the silver punch-marked and the tribal coins.[9] The symbol is absent in the epigraphs of subsequent periods.

A form quite similar to it is noticed in the graffiti in Harappan and Megalithic pottery but the symbol is engraved like the Greek letter alpha (α).[10] As a potter's mark it might have had a long life, for a *ma*-like symbol occurs frequently on the historical pottery.[11]

(ii) *Symbol looking like ram's head:* Only one example of this symbol is so far known. It is noticed in one of the inscriptions from Kuda (fig. 2, *9*) where the mark is incised at the end of the epigraph. It has a trapezoidal body surmounted by a semi-circular line with curled ends. Symbols appearing on the early coins and in the graffiti on pottery do not include this form.

(iii) *Two-limbed symbols*: Represented by about seven examples, the symbol is restricted to western India. Three of them come from Kuda; those found at Junnar and Kol show a much stylized form. The one from Mahad is very similar to those found at Kuda.

The symbol has more or less a triangular appearance with lateral sides curved in opposite direction. At Kuda (fig. 2, *1-3*) itself two different forms are noticed: two of them are surmounted by a row of minute triangles varying in number, either five or seven (fig. 2, *2, 3*) and the third one (fig. 2, *1*) without this feature. Mahad differs in having a dotted line on the top (fig. 2, *4*) instead of a triangle-topped one. At Junnar (fig. 2, *5*) though the sides have become fully concave, it retains all other essential features. The example from Kol (fig. 2, *10*) is, however, far removed from any other specimen in so far as its form is concerned: it has only two concave sides with a vertical line running in between. It may even be termed as a three-limbed symbol; *vajra* in Indra's hand is quite similar to it. Except in one case from Junnar where it occupies a place at the end of the first line, all other examples are found at the opening of the inscriptions. At Mahad, it occurs along with a *triratna* above the inscription.

The symbol appears to have no parallel in the collection of symbols on ancient Indian coins and graffiti on pottery. It looks like a conventionalized representation of a bunch of corn tied together.

(iv) *Two-pronged symbol:* The only example of this variety is from Kailvan, district Patna (*EI*, XXXI, pp. 229-231). This symbol (fig. 2, *31*) is formed by means of two curved arms joined by a horizontal line at the base which is supported by a pole with a knob near the bottom. The symbol may be termed as representing a two-pronged standard. It is vaguely reminiscent of a symbol of an earlier occurrence from Sohagaura (fig. 1, *2*, no. 5) (see above, pp. 8-9) which, however, is without the pole.

B. Triskelion and *triratna*

The group includes (i) simple triskelion, (ii) snake symbol inside a crescent, and (iii) *triratna*. Broadly speaking, three-limbed and three-pronged symbols are included under this category.

(i) *Simple triskelion*: The triskelion, a three-limbed symbol, occurs only twice in inscriptions (fig. 1, *1*, nos. 3-5). Some scholars take it as a modified form of *svastika,*[12] but it is a very ancient and widespread symbol[13] and has also been used in the silver punch-marked and uninscribed coins. Surprisingly, it is not to be found in Allan's list of symbols on tribal coins. As already stated, the symbol is confined only to the Aśokan inscriptions.

(ii) *Snake symbol inside a crescent*: The correct interpretation of this symbol can only be guessed. On the analogy of symbols appearing on ancient

Fig. 3. Early symbols: 1 Hathigumpha; 2 Bhaja; 3 Bedsa; 4 Karle; 5 Junnar; 6-7 Jankhat;. 8-11 Kuda; 12-13 Taxila; 14-17 Junnar; 18 Mahad; 19-21 Amaravati; 22-24 Tribal coins; 25 Kuda

coins, the hook-like object may be taken as representing snake,[14] and the semi-circular one as crescent. The combined picture gives the appearance of a three-limbed figure.

The symbol occurs at the opening of the inscriptions from Bhaja and Karle (fig. 2, *23-24*), the latter representation is in double lines. It seems to have had a short span of life and is not found outside northern Deccan.

(iii) *Triratna*: Basically it is a three-pronged symbol; the name *triratna* is given to this form because of its strong association with the Buddhist sites. But for the upward prongs the similarity between the different examples is very little.

Of the eighteen examples collected here from various inscriptions, only five have come from outside the western Indian group of caves. Its popularity in western India is next only to the *svastika*, about twenty-seven examples of which are known from the cave-inscriptions.

The symbol[15] occurs at the opening of the records at Bhaja, Bedsa, Junnar and Karle (fig. 3, *2-5*). In Hathigumpha inscription of Khāravela (fig. 3, *1*; pl. II), it occupies the top left margin of the inscription. But at Kuda (fig. 3, *8-11*) and Amaravati (fig. 3, *20*) the symbol is generally placed at the end of the record (pl. I C). The symbol occurs twice in the same inscription from Junnar—at the beginning of both lines 1 and 2. On a comparatively late inscription from Jankhat (fig. 3, *7*), a three-pronged symbol occurs on either side of a tree, all of them being depicted above the inscription (*EI*, XI, p. 85).

The variety of forms makes it difficult to attempt a classification of this popular symbol. So far as the top is concerned it may be blunted, pointed, barbed and hooded. Even the base is variable as it may be circular, semi-circular, concave or pronged. The most ornate type is found at Amaravati[16] where it marks the end of the epigraph, while conventionalized forms are represented in inscriptions from Bedsa, Junnar and Kuda. In certain varieties, one can notice tentacle-like feature on either sides of the symbol; in one instance, the tentacles are replaced by dots.

Taking all these variable features into consideration one may divide the three-pronged or three-headed symbols into five broad sub-types, viz., (a) those with slightly constricted waist and two rounded heads; (b) those of elongated or oblong variety with semi-circular or concave base; (c) those with tentacles or protuberance on either side; (d) those where tentacles are replaced by dots; and (e) those where both tentacles and dots are absent. Examples of sub-type (a) are found at Hathigumpha, Junnar and Jankhat; one of the examples from Junnar bears close resemblance with the one noticed in the Hathigumpha inscription. In this variety neither the tentacles nor the dots are shown. Sub-type (b) differs from the above in having an elongated or oblong body. Examples of this category are noticed at Bhaja, Karle and Amaravati (fig. 3, *2, 4, 21*). On the ground of similarity of convex base the ornamental example from Amaravati may also be included in this sub-type. Those with protuberances or tentacles appear to be a characteristic type which is noticed in the inscriptions from Kuda and Junnar. This form has its counterpart even outside India and is also noticed on certain varieties of tribal coins (fig. 3, *23-24*). Save one example, all other specimens from Kuda conform to this sub-type (c). Of the six specimens from Junnar, four belong to this variety. It includes also a symbol with duplication of three prongs, placed one above the other. Sub-type (d) is represented by a single example from Kuda. It occurs also on the tribal coins and on a square copper seal from Taxila (fig. 3, *13*) (*CII*, II, i, p. 101, pl. XX, 9). The last sub-type (e) is noticed in the inscriptions from Bedsa and Junnar. An almost similar symbol is also found on an inscribed gold ring from Taxila (fig. 3, *13*) (*CII*, II, i, p. 100, pl. XX, 1).

Surprisingly, the three-pronged symbol was hardly used in the inscriptions of the later period. But whatever may be its beginning, the symbol continued to be commonly used by the Buddhists, Jainas and certain Brahmanical sects, though, of course, under different sectarian names. It appears from the evidence of inscriptions and coins that the three-pronged symbol either as *triratna* or *nandipāda* became popular only during the early Christian era.

C. Triangular variety of symbols

Under this head it is proposed to deal with the following three symbols, viz., (i) triangular-headed standard, (ii) *ḍamaru,* and (iii) sacrificial post. In all these symbols the triangular form appears to be the most important.

(i) *Triangular-headed standard*: The earliest evidence of triangular headed standard comes from an inscription in the Udayagiri-Khandagiri caves ascribable to the first century BC (fig. 2, *11*; pl. I D); sometimes it has been identified as tree-within-railing. But as the symbol does not show any leaf or branch it is more appropriate to call it a standard. Further, a vertical line bisects the triangle supported on a standard which is covered by a barred rail.

The inscriptions of the Udayagiri-Khandagiri group of caves show a predilection for this symbol, for a slightly different form of the triangular standard occurs in the Manchapuri and Bagh caves (fig. 2, *12, 13*), both being slightly later than the Hathigumpha inscription chronologically. In the last-mentioned inscription the symbol is at the end while it is incised at the beginning of the inscriptions from Bagh and Manchapuri (*EI*, XIII, p. 159). R.D. Banerjee makes the following observation while editing the inscription from Bagh caves: "The inscription begins with a symbol which resembles one of the symbols on the lower part of one of the pillars found in the recent excavations at Pāṭaliputra, which is a modification of the *crux ansata* or the Egyptian symbol of life. It ends with a regular well-formed *Svastika mark.*"

Whether the symbol bears a comparison with the Egyptian symbol of life is debatable; it is however frequently represented on the ancient Indian coins. Those appearing on silver punch-marked coins and uninscribed cast coins have railing around the standard; the type continues even in the coins of Kausambi, Ujjain and Taxila. A form very similar to the one depicted on some Ujjain coins bears comparison with the standard incised at the end of the Hathigumpha inscription. Likewise, the Bagh example may be compared with a coin-device from Eran. In case of Bagh a five-barred rail surrounds the standard. The triangular top shows three horizontal bars projecting to the right; its top is open like the one appearing on the inscription from the Manchapuri cave. In case of the latter the horizontal bars are, however, distributed on both sides—two on the left and one on the right. But Manchapuri example does not show any rail around the pole.

An interesting variety of this symbol comes from the Gunji rock-inscription (fig. 2, *14*) of Kumāravaradatta (*EI*, XXVII, p. 48) ascribable to the first century AD. It is double-lined with top decorated by means of a row of small triangles, five in number. Just below the top of the inverted triangle is to be seen an outgrowth possibly representing the lingering vestige of the horizontal bar so common on the coin devices. Its decoration on the top reminds one of the identical designs on some of the symbols from Kuda, Mahad and Junnar.

(ii) *Ḍamaru*: The symbol comprises two isosceles triangles meeting at the apex, with a horizontal bar at the point of intersection; its similarity with *ḍamaru* or drum may be superficial, and not real. The symbol appears five times in different inscriptions from Karle, Kuda and Nasik. A solitary example of this symbol in eastern India can also be seen from Kailvan (fig. 2, *22*) in district Patna (*EI*, XXXI, pp. 229-231) where it occurs as one of the symbols in a sequence in an inscription datable to AD 186. In four inscriptions the symbol appears at the opening, and the outline is more or less uniform, but in one of the examples from Karle it marks the end of the record.

The symbol is rarely represented on the coins; the only coin-device which approximates the design in the inscriptions is from Ayodhya. Yet it seems to be an ancient and widely-distributed symbol in India, for, similar representation without, however, the horizontal bar, is found in the graffiti on pottery from Harappan, chalcolithic and megalithic sites.[17] But exact parallel is from Nagarjunakonda where it occurs as a mason's mark.[18] Evidently, the drum-symbol with a horizontal bar in the centre is a distinct variety which might not have any bearing on the symbol occuring as a graffiti. And this evolved shape might have emerged in the west coast some time in the early Christian era.

(iii) *Sacrificial post*: In the triangular-headed standard the apex is at the bottom but in case of sacrificial post the triangle has its apex pointing upwards. The symbol appears to be a naturalistic representation of a sacrificial post or *yūpa*. After the numeral 90, almost in the centre of the last line is found the symbol on one of the two *yūpa* inscriptions from (fig. 2, *27*) Barnala (*EI*, XXVI, p. 119); it is very similar to the one depicted on the Badva *yūpa* inscription A.

D. Miscellaneous symbols

Different types of symbols have been included under this group which may further be sub-divided into eight sub-types.

(a) *Tree-within-railing and other plant devices*: There are two definite representations of tree-within-railing on the Sohagaura copper-plate of the third century BC. In fact, the series starts with the tree-within-railing symbol; it has only three leaves drooping in three directions (fig. 1, *2*, no. 1). A leafless plant is also represented as the sixth device on the plate. The leafless tree capped as if by a two-pronged symbol has an elaborate three-barred rail (fig. 1, *2*, no. 6); its main stem inclining towards the right pointing to a double-roofed structure identified as granary. The third symbol may be taken as a bud although it looks like a spoon with a long handle (fig. 1, *2,* no. 3). Bühler considered it to be a toilet-mirror. On some variety of the punch-marked silver coins is found a spoon-like object—similar to the one depicted on the Sohagaura plate flanked on either side by taurine symbol. The other two trees have no exact parallel in the repository of symbols on Indian coins.

Apart from the plants drawn on the Sohagaura plate there is another representation of tree on the Jankhat inscription (fig. 2, *29*; pl. I B) of the time of Vīrasena, AD 300 (*EI*, XI, p. 85). No railing was provided around the tree which seems to be a crudely-executed one.

(b) *Hill surmounted by crescent*: The symbol, a popular device on ancient Indian coins, is found only on the Sohagaura plate (fig. 1, *2*, no. 4). It is a three-arched symbol with a dot above the crescent. Generally, the form is represented on coins without dot and Allan's lists of symbols on punch-marked, cast and tribal coins do not show this minute dot. Yet, a perusal of the published plates will leave no doubt as to its existence in some cases.

For instance, the dot surrounded by a crescent is to be seen on the coins in Plate XI, 20 and 24 of Allan.[19]

(c) *Structural representations*: It is the Sohagaura inscription again which supplies the evidence of structural representations on inscriptions (fig. 1, *2*, nos. 2 and 7). The second and the seventh devices on the plate are those of structures, with curved double roof—the lower roof supported by four and the upper and the smaller one by three front posts. They have three pinnacles on top and seem to have a naturalistic form.

A symbol simulating an altar is found at the opening of two inscriptions from Kuda. In both the cases the symbol has a splayed-out top with a ridged shaft and expanded base. One of the symbols, however, shows three circular objects placed above.

The Nasik inscription of Vāśishṭhiputra Pulumāyī ends with a three-pronged conical object, the exact nature of which is difficult to find out

(d) *Animal figure*: Despite the fact that taurine symbol was used from a very early period the occurrence of animal figures on early inscriptions is extremely rare. One doubtful example—possibly the figure of a lion—is noticed at the beginning of an inscription from Kuda (fig. 2, *32*).

(e) *Water-vessel*: The lone example of this variety is from Kailvan (fig. 2, *30* and fig. 1, *4*, no. 1), district Patna (*EI*, XXXI, pp. 229-31) where it appears as the first symbol in a group of five. It has a long, straight neck, globular body and pedestal base. Since it appears as the first symbol, it might be signifying perhaps a *pūrṇa-ghaṭa*, a *maṅgala*.

(f) *Indeterminate symbols*: There are two symbols the nature of which cannot be guessed. The one appearing on the Sohagaura plate is a simple U-shaped symbol with a dot below (fig. 1, *2*, no. 5). Some scholars have read it as *mo*, although it is difficult to agree to this view. This is the only symbol on the Sohagaura plate which does not stand in the same alignment as that of the rest.

The other symbol looks like a pattern and occurs at the beginning of an inscription from Kuda (fig. 3, *25*). On the Gunji rock inscription of Kumāravaradatta, referred to above, occurs another ornamental figure alongside the one already described but it is very much defaced, and hence, difficult to restore.

It is evident from the foregoing that about a score of symbols occur in the early inscriptions, majority of which are from western India. Some symbols, especially those appearing on the Aśokan edicts, Sohagaura plate, Rampurva copper belt and on the cave-inscriptions from Orissa are comparable to the symbols on the early coins. On the other hand, majority of marks on the cave-inscriptions from western India seem to have no mooring and might have come into existence during the early Christian era.

Either the symbols were evolved there or were introduced into India in the trail of foreign contact. Symbols looking like ram's head, *ḍamaru,* altar, orbed conical object, lion, representation simulating a bunch of corn tied together are some of the forms which have rarely been used as auspicious marks in ancient India. Yet their abrupt appearance was accompanied by equally sudden absence; but for the *triratna* and the *svastika,* all other symbols soon fell into disuse, thereby suggesting their impervious character. But this aspect of Indian symbolism will be discussed separately in Chapter 3.

Notes and References

1. F.R. Allchin, 'Upon the contextual significance of certain groups of ancient Indian signs', *Bulletin of the School of Oriental and African Studies,* University of London, XXII (1959), pp. 541-555.
2. For the list of different publications on the inscription, see D.C. Sircar, *Select Inscriptions bearing on Indian History and Civilization* (Calcutta, 1965), I, p. 82.
3. J. Allan, in his *Catalogue of the Coins of ancient India in the British Museum* (London, 1936), p. xxii writes: 'A striking feature about the symbols on the silver punch-marked coins is the complete absence of some well-known Indian symbols very common on other series of coins, such as the *svastika* and simple triskeles, the so-called Ujjain symbol in its various forms, and the Nandipāda so common in more or less elaborate forms elsewhere, the hollow cross common at Taxila'. Also see, Parmeshwari Lal Gupta, *Punch-Marked Coins in the Andhra Pradesh Government Museum,* Andhra Pradesh Museum Series, No. 1 (Hyderabad, 1961), pl. I, no. 51, pl. II, nos. 113-115, 137-140, for examples of triskelion with taurine symbols on punch-marked coins.
4. Allchin, *op.cit.*, p. 553, thinks that "the copper bolt from Rāmpurvā must bear marks put on it at that time [i.e., the Mauryan period] probably by the royal coppersmiths." He also suggests that "in particular the ubiquitous hill-with-crescent sign, recurring throughout, may have something of the significance of the mark of a far-reaching authority, extending at least from Patna to Taxila, and impressing itself upon the products of stone-masons, coppersmiths, copper and silver coiners, potters, etc. Such a mark may be expected to be a royal or dynastic sign (Kauṭilya's *rājāṅka* or *narendrāṅka)* as Jayaswal and Prasad long ago opined. If indeed it has that significance then it can only belong to the Mauryan dynasty or at least to a single ruler thereof." Allchin, *op.cit.*, pp. 554-555, further points out that "the Rāmpurvā copper bolt and the Kumrahar pillar base bear groups of marks indicating the authority which caused then to he made. This authority can only have been that of a Mauryan ruler, either Chandragupta, Bindusāra or Aśoka".

5. Jas. Burgess, *Report on the Buddhist Cave Temples and their Inscriptions*, Archaeological Survey of Western India, Vol. IV (London, 1883), pls. XLIV-LV.
6. For variations in the position of different symbols, see Burgess, *ibid.*
7. D.C. Sircar (1965) *Select Inscriptions*, *op.cit.*, pl. XXXVII.
8. It has been suggested by J.N. Banerjea that the taurine symbol "might symbolise the sun and the moon represented together, the disc symbolising the former, the latter being symbolised by the crescent attached to it"; see, J.N. Banerjea, *The Development of Hindu Iconography* (Calcutta, 1956), p. 138.
9. Allan, *op.cit.*, pp. 300 and 308.
10. B.B. Lal, 'From the Megalithic to the Harappa: Tracing back the graffiti on the pottery', *Ancient India*, no. 16 (1960), pl. XXII A.
11. For example it is noticed on the pottery from Stratum VIII (BC 300-200) of Ahichchhatrā. See, A. Ghosh and K.C. Panigrahi, 'Pottery of Ahichchhatrā (U.P.)', *Ancient India*, no. 1 (Jan. 1946), p. 52, fig. 7, no. 2.
12. D.C. Sircar, *Indian Epigraphy* (Delhi, 1965), p. 93.
13. Donald A. Mackenzie in his *The Migration of Symbols* (London, 1926), p. 155 writes: 'It may have originally symbolized the three seasons of the early agriculturists of Egypt—the hot season, the cool season and the season of inundation, represented by the lion-headed goddess, the cow goddess and the hippopotamus goddess as in the Tutankhamen's tomb. The three-limbed symbol may have represented the earth, air and sky—the deities Geb, Shu 'and Nut'. Mackenzie has published the drawing of a triskelion occurring on the coin from Megara: the symbol bears close resemblance with that found in India. It is also found at certain sites from Minoan levels; see, Arthur J. Evans, *Scripta Minoa*, I (Oxford, 1909), p. 121, fig. 54.
14. M.C. Joshi, 'Kuninda Coinage: A Review', *Bharatiya Vidya*, XXII, nos. 1 to 4 (1962) takes, after J.N. Banerjea, *op.cit.*, the symbol as *śrivatsa*.
15. *Triratna* occurs in sculptural representations at Bharhut; see, Alexander Cunningham, *The Stupa of Bharhut* (London, 1879), pl. L.7 (similar to the Bhaja and Karle examples in fig. 3, *2, 4*).
16. C. Sivaramamurti, *Amaravati Scultpures in the Madras Government Museum* (Madras, 1956), pl. IV, 35 and 38.
17. Lal, *op.cit.* (1960), pl. XXXII, 1.
18. Sarkar (in press).
19. Allan, *op.cit.* (1936).

CHAPTER 3

THE SVASTIKA

Widely known by its Sanskrit name, the *svastika* is still a living symbol—a symbol of sanctity and auspiciousness. It is of considerable antiquity[1] and occurs in almost all parts of the globe. In India, its antiquity dates back to the Harappan times; it has been used in a variety of ways and has acquired a variety of meanings. Its occurrence in early inscriptions, therefore, is not unusual. As a matter of fact, the *svastika* was one of the earliest auspicious marks that made its way into the Indian epigraphs. But it seems to have attained maximum proliferation in epigraphs only during the early centuries of the Christian era, and has been used less often in the inscriptions of later times.

The earliest use of *svastika* in an inscription is in the Jaugada version of the two separate edicts of Aśoka[2] (fig. 4, *1, 2*). Both the *vāma-āvarta* and the *dakshiṇa-āvarta* types[3] occur along with taurine symbols.[4] On the left hand side margin of the Hathigumpha cave inscription of Khāravela (fig. 4, *3*; pl. II) is also found a *svastika.*[5] Several cave-inscriptions from Bhaja, Junnar, Kanheri, Karle, Kuda and Nasik[6] (fig. 4, *6-13*) have yielded this symbol, which is also noticed at Amaravati (fig. 4, *4*) (*EI*, XV, p. 24), Bagh cave in the Udayagiri hills, Orissa (fig. 4, *4*) (*EI*, XIII, p. 159), Mora well inscription from Mathura (fig. 4, *5*; pl. IV A) (*EI*, XXIV, p. 194) and Peshawar (fig. 4, *16*) (*EI*, XIX, p. 202). All the inscriptions mentioned above are engraved on rock or stone, and range in date from the first to the third centuries AD. The latest known example (fig. 4, *18*) is in the copper-plate grant of the Reḍḍis of Kondavidu, dated to AD 1380 (*EI*, III, p. 59); it appears to be an isolated example in that period. Perhaps it may reasonably be emphasized here that *svastika* as an auspicious mark was incised generally in the early inscriptions, majority of them hailing either from Buddhist or Jaina centres; the latter included sites like Mathura, Hathigumpha and Bagh caves in the Udayagiri-Khandagiri hills.

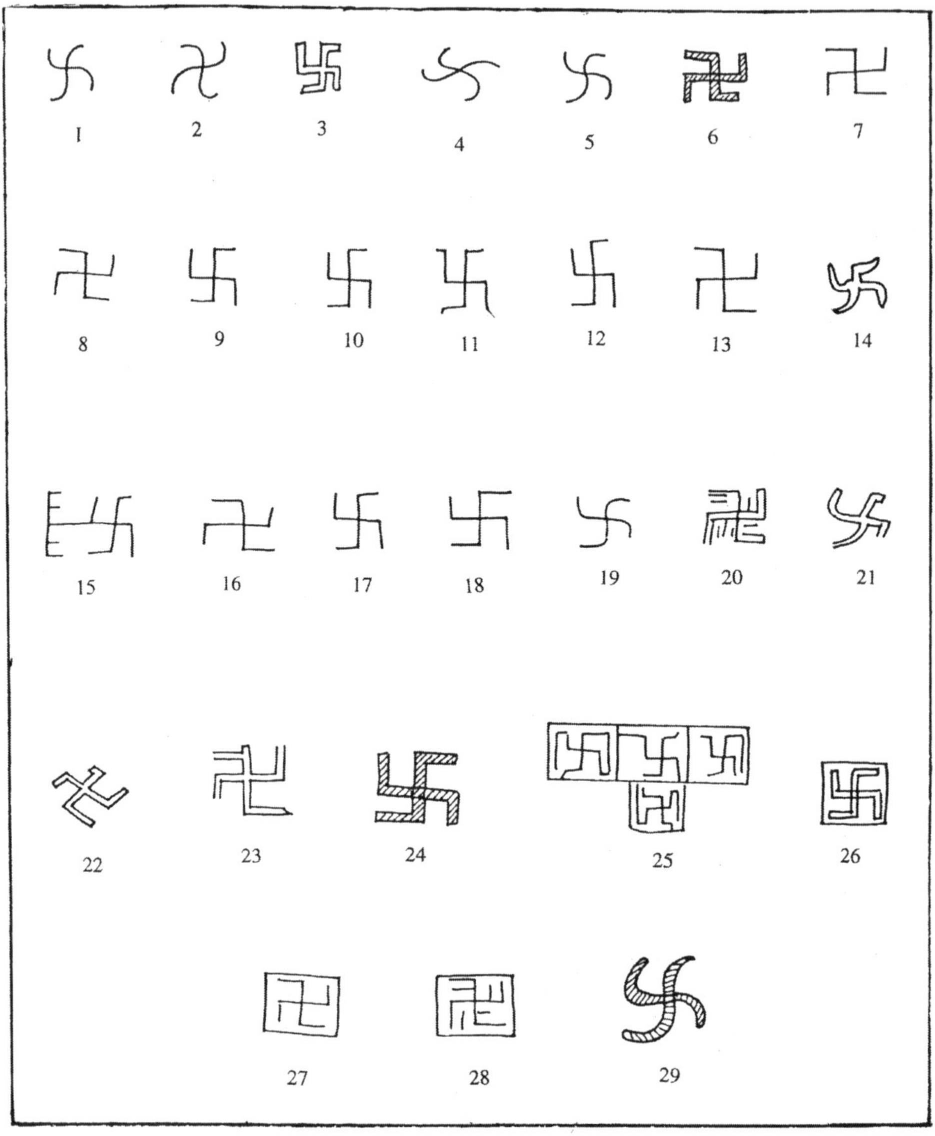

Fig. 4. *Svastika*: 1-2 Jaugada; 3 Hathigumpha; 4 Amaravati; 5 Mathura; 6-8 Kuda; 9 Nasik; 10-11 Karle; 12-13 Junnar; 14 Udayagiri, Orissa; 15 Sri Lanka; 16 Peshawar; 17 Kolur; 18 Kondavidu; 19 Hastināpura, Period II, on pottery; 20 Hastināpura, Period IV, on pottery; 21-22; Rupar, first-second century AD, on pottery; 23 Arikamedu, second century AD, on pottery; 24 Ahichchhatrā, 200-100 BC, on pottery; 25-27 Harappa, seal; 28 Mohenjo-daro seal; 29 Shahi Tump

The position of the *svastika* in an inscription does not follow a set pattern. But generally it is found at the commencement or at the conclusion or at both the places (pl. III). Regarding the position of the symbol in the Jaugada edict, Hultzsch makes the following observation: "The separation of these two edicts is more distinctly marked by the accompaniment of the *svastika* symbol at each of the upper corners of the upper inscription, and of the letter *ma* at the upper corners of the lower inscription".[7] In the Peshawar Museum inscription of the year 168 (*CII*, II, p. 77) the symbol is placed below the inscription while in some inscriptions from Amaravati (fig. 4, *4*), Junnar, Kanheri, Karle, Kuda and in the Bagh cave in Orissa, the *svastika* marks the end of the epigraph. In some instances from Bhaja, Junnar, Kanheri, Kuda and Nasik, inscriptions open with the symbol although several other (see Chapter 4) symbols have also been used for the purpose. The third series comprises those examples, where the *svastika* is engraved not only at the beginning but also at the end of the same epigraph: examples of this category come from Junnar and Karle. Nasik provides a case of interesting variation of position of the symbol; in one example *svastika* precedes the word *siddhaṁ*, whereas in another the symbol follows the same word.

An interesting fact emerges from the foregoing discussion: the symbol became very popular in western India during the early centuries of the Christian era.[8] In fact, it is the area of high incidence of the *svastika* symbol so far as its occurrence in inscriptions is concerned. In other areas, during the same epoch, they occur only sporadically. The *svastika* as a coin-device possibly became popular only during this time, as it occurs in the copper cast coins and in different issues which are collectively known as tribal coins including the local varieties. Allan's *Catalogue* does not include the *svastika* in the list of symbols on the punch-marked coins.[9] It is, therefore, not unlikely that the period of popularity of the *svastika* as a coin-device would coincide more or less with that of the inscription: the period begins from Khāravela's time to about the beginning of the third century.[10]

The *svastika* engraved in different inscriptions does not conform to a uniform type. Broadly, the symbol may be divided into four distinct varieties, viz., (i) ogee *svastika*, (fig. 4, *1, 2, 4* and *5*), (ii) those of equal-limbed variety (fig. 4, *7-13, 16-18*), (iii) the hollow (fig. 4, *3, 14*), and (iv) blocked varieties (fig. 4; *6*). Those found in the Jaugada version of the two separate rock-edicts of Aśoka belong to the ogee type (pl. III). It occurs in the Amaravati[11] and the Mathura inscriptions also, but this series, obvious as it is, has to be distinguished chronologically from the Aśokan one. In the sculptures of Amaravati and Nagarjunkonda *svastika* is generally represented by its ogee form. It may be recorded here that ogee *svastikas* have greater antiquity, for, they are found painted on the pottery from Shahi Tump[12] (fig. 4, *29*), protohistoric site in Baluchistan and from Hastinapura (fig. 4, *19*) from the Painted Grey Ware levels (c. 1100-800 BC).[13] But the type is rare in Harappa culture. However, a type quite nearer to the ogee variety is to be seen as graffito on the chalcolithic pottery from Navdatoli and Rangpur.[14] At Rupar,[15] district Ambala, and Ahichchhatrā,[16] district Bareilly (U.P.) can also be seen examples of the ogee variety of *svastika* on the pottery belonging to the early centuries of the Christian era (fig. 4, 21). On early coins, this form is confined to certain varieties of the Taxila issues.[17] The ogee form of *svastika*[18] seems to have at least three different periods of its popularity: (a) the period before the first millennium BC, (b) during the third century BC, and (c) in the early Christian eras, the last two phases being represented by symbols appearing in the inscriptions.

Type ii appears to be the most widely distributed *svastika*, and is noticed in the inscriptions from western India, Orissa and Peshawar. The *svastika* from the Udayagiri cave, Orissa, (fig. 4, *14*), has somewhat curved arms and the one from Karle (fig. 4, 11) has hooked ends in three of its four limbs. This type occurs on the uninscribed cast and tribal coins as well.

Type iii is represented by a solitary specimen from the Hathigumpha inscription of Khāravela (fig. 4, *3*). But this variety is frequently noticed in the Harappan sites[19] (fig. 4, *26*), and perhaps also as graffiti on the megalithic pottery.[20] It is used either as a painted, impressed or incised design on the pottery from Taxila (Sirkap),[21] Ahichchhatrā[22] and Arikamedu[23] (fig. 4, *23, 24*). The sherd bearing the *svastika* from the last-named site is of the rouletted ware and the *svastika* is 'cut on the outside after firing'.[24] Type iv is also represented by a lone example occurring in one of the inscriptions from Kuda (fig. 4, *6*). It is also represented on the pottery from Stratum VII (BC 200-100) from Ahichchhatra[25] (fig. 4, *24*). Both Types iii and iv are basically of equal-limbed variety.

Mention may be made of a peculiar type of *svastika* in an early inscription from Sri Lanka (*IA*, I, p. 139) belonging to Devānāmpiya Tissa (fig. 4, *15*). In this specimen, the *svastika* is joined by a horizontal stroke with a vertical line having five bars including the connecting line, all being to its right. It appears like a combination of two symbols, a *svastika* and a five-barred vertical shaft. A three-barred symbol appears side by side *svastika* on some Ujjayini coins;[26] 'a vertical line joined by a series of horizontal stroke' is found amongst the graffiti on Indian pottery of different periods.[27] Combination of more than one symbol giving rise to a monogrammatic form is however not rare; a typical example is a *svastika* with taurine symbol at the end of arms. *Svastikas* inside the circles of the

Ujjain symbol is also a well-known coin-device. Thus *svastikas* have been used in Indian symbolism in combination with other symbols, although their occurrence in Indian inscriptions is not reported as yet.

It appears from the study of *svastika* that the symbol has been used as an auspicious mark not only in the epigraphs, but also on coins, as graffiti on pottery, in seals and also as a favourite motif in the decoration of some protohistoric pottery. So far as its occurrence in inscriptions is concerned it reveals different periods of rise and fall in its popularity. The ogee form reappeared, for a brief spell, in the Aśokan edicts after remaining dormant for a millennium or so. The next period of its rise, this time in the Buddhist sites on the eastern sea-board, took place in the early centuries of the Christian era, when it was adopted also as a coin-device. Those of the equal-limbed variety became popular in inscriptions and coins in the period beginning from the second-first centuries BC to about the third century AD. In this period the form made its impact in the art and architecture of the time as well: there are cases where *svastika* was placed in the centre of some *stūpas* at Nagarjunakonda.[28] Evidently, the symbol was transformed into an art-motif, invested with some philosophical import. During this long lease of life, the symbol seems to have typified some sort of syncretic qualities as is evident from coin-devices and the combined form incised on a Simhalese record. All this change, all this rise and fall in the popularity of this symbol in India, may portray corresponding change in the philosophical outlook due to the rise of new ideology or contact with culture.

Notes and References

1. Thomas Wilson in his *The Swastika* (Washington, 1876), p. 768 propounds the theory of west Asian origin of the symbol. A.K. Coomaraswamy also holds a similar view. See his *History of Indian and Indonesian Art* (London, 1927), pp. 13-14, 44.
2. E. Hultzsch, *Inscriptions of Aśoka*, Corpus Inscriptionum Indicarum, I (Oxford, 1925), plate facing p. 116.
3. "Prof Max Muller makes the symbol different according as the arms are bent to the right or to the left. That bent to the right he denominates the true Swastika, that bent to the left he calls Suavastika". See, Wilson, *op.cit.*, p. 767.
4. Hultzsch and Harit Krishna Deb take the symbol as Brāhmī *ma*. The latter explains the *svastika* as a monogram consisting of two Brāhmī O's and the *ma* as the final letter of the sacred syllable *Oṁ*. See, Harit Krishna Deb, 'The Svastika and the Oṁkāra', *Journal and Proceedings of the Asiatic Society of Bengal*, New Series, Vol. XVII (1921), p. 231. Cunningham also

regards it as a monogram combining the letters of the auspicious words *su asti (svasti)* in Aśokan Brāhmī. For this and other theories on the origin of the symbol, see 'Notes on the *Swastika*' by R. Sewell in the *Indian Antiquary*, X (1881), p. 199, which was based on the earlier contributions in the same journal by S. Beal, E. Thomas, Walhouse, etc. See *Indian Antiquary*, VII (1878), p. 176; IX (1880), p. 65; also see, H.G.M. Murray-Aynsley, 'Discursive contributions towards the Comparative Study of Asiatic Symbolism', XV (1886) pp. 61 ff. Also Donald A. Mackenzie, *The Migration of Symbols* (London, 1926), pp. 1-46.

5. D.C. Sircar, *Select Inscriptions bearing on Indian History and Civilization,* (1965), p. 214, pl. XXXVII.
6. Jas. Burgess, *Report on the Buddhist Cave Temples and their Inscriptions*, Archaeological Survey of Western India, Vol. IV (London, 1883), pp. 82-107.
7. Hultzsch, *op.cit.* (1925), p. xiv.
8. D.C. Sircar, *op.cit.* (1965), p. 93. According to him, "the *svastika* is also found at the beginning and the end of many other records generally belonging to dates earlier than the 3rd century AD".
9. John Allan, *A Catalogue of the Indian Coins in the British Museum* (London, 1936), pp. 297-309.
10. For chronology of cast copper and tribal coins, see Allan, *ibid.*, pp. lxxvii ff.
11. C. Sivaramamurti, *Amaravati Sculptures in the Madras Government Museum* (Madras, 1956), pl. IV.
12. Aurel Stein, *An Archaeological Tour in Gedrosia*, Memoirs of the Archaeological Survey of India, no. 43 (Calcutta, 1931), pl. XV.
13. B.B. Lal, 'Excavations at Hastinapura and other Explorations in the Upper Gaṅga and Sutlej Basins', *Ancient India*, nos. 10 & 11 (1954 & 1955), pl. XXIV, no. 4, p. 34.
14. B.B. Lal 'From the Megalithic to the Harappa: Tracing back the Graffiti on the pottery', *Ancient India*, no. 16 (1960), p. 12, pl. XIV.
15. Y.D. Sharma, 'Exploration of Historical Sites', *Ancient India,* no. 9 (1953), p. 129, fig. 7.
16. A. Ghosh and K.C. Panigrahi, 'The pottery of Ahichchhatra, dist. Bareilly, U.P.', *Ancient India*, no. 1 (Jan. 1946), p. 53, fig. 8, nos. 15 and 16.
17. Allan, *op.cit.,* pp. cxxxvii, 233 and 236.
18. It is an oft-repeated symbol on the Trojan whorls. See Mackenzie, *op.cit.,* pp. 809-833, figs. 41-87.
19. Sir John Marshall, *Mohenjo-daro and the Indus Civilization* (London, 1931), III, pl. CXIV; E.J.H. Mackay, *Further Excavations at Mohenjo-daro* (Delhi, 1937), II, pls. LXXXII to LXXXVIII, XCI, XCIV, XCVIII and *CII*; M.S. Vats, *Excavations at Harappa* (Delhi, 1940), II, pls. XCII and XCV.
20. B.B. Lal, *op.cit.,* p. 12.
21. A. Ghosh, 'Taxila (Sirkap) 1944-5', *Ancient India*, no. 4 (July 1947-January 1948), pp. 70-71, fig. 17, XLI.

22. A. Ghosh and K.C. Panigrahi, *op.cit.* (1946), p. 52.
23. R.E.M. Wheeler, A. Ghosh and Krishna Deva, 'Arikamedu: an Indo-Roman Trading Station on the East Coast of India', *Ancient India*, no. 2 (July, 1946), pp. 47, 49, fig. 12, 1g.
24. Wheeler, *et al., ibid.*, p. 47.
25. A. Ghosh and K.C. Panigrahi, *op.cit.* (1946), p. 52.
26. Allan, *op.cit.*, pp. 241, 258-259.
27. B.B. Lal, *op.cit.*, p. 12. Such a symbol occurs also on the Trojan whorls. Parallelism shown in this and other case is only a superficial comparison, and does not aim at giving any pointer.
28. H. Sarkar, *Studies in Early Buddhist Architecture of India* (New Delhi, 1966), p. 90.

CHAPTER 4

SUPPOSED SYMBOL FOR *'OṀ'* OR *'SIDDHAṀ'*

Of all the symbols, the one supposedly representing *Oṁ* or *Siddhaṁ* is the most common in Indian epigraphs. It has been used in the early period generally at the commencement of the inscriptions, but in later times the practice of inscribing the symbol at the end or even several times within the main text also assumed wide currency, especially in the Karnataka region (below, p. 33). In some Sālaṅkāyana grants the symbol stands also on the margin.

The history of the development of this symbol covers a period of about a millennium and a half, and in space the entire sub-continent. The pattern of development, however, follows a multilateral course, sometimes with marked regional variations.[1] It has at least thirty-one variants and all of them might have sprung from a common source. Despite apparent dissimilarities, there pervades an underlying unity amongst the different variable forms.

1. Classification

Broadly speaking, these symbols in the first instance, may be divided into two groups, Variant 1 (fig. 5) and Variant 2 (fig. 6). While the actual number of sub-varities may be much more, we have been able to identify respectively in Variant 1 and Variant 2, sixteen and fifteen sub-varieties, including the prototypes. Symbols generally drawn from left to right or with their mouths turned to (spectator's) right (*dakṣhiṇa-āvarta*) are included under Variant 1, while those drawn in the reverse direction *(vāma-āvarta)* fall under Variant 2. It is proposed here to deal with each of the sub-varieties separately.

Variant 1: The original prototype: (fig. 5) The earliest example of the symbol turned to the right dates back to AD 81-82 of Kanishka's reign (*EI*, XXXIV, p. 9). It is more or less an L-shaped mark used in the opening of the epigraph discovered at Mathura. The symbol has been equated with

PERIOD OF EMERGENCE			VARIANT 1
1	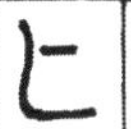	1st CENTURY	MATHURA
1a		3rd CENTURY	NAGARJUNAKONDA
1b		5th CENTURY	ANDHRA, ORISSA, CENTRAL INDIA, ASSAM, TAMIL NADU
1c		4th CENTURY	GUJARAT, MADHYA PRADESH, ANDHRA, BIHAR
1d		4th-5th CENTURY	MAHARASHTRA, KARNATAKA, ANDHRA, MADHYA PRADESH
1e		8th CENTURY	KARNATAKA, GUJARAT, ANDHRA
1f		11th CENTURY	KARNATAKA
1g		7th CENTURY	ORISSA, BENGAL, ANDHRA, MAHARASHTRA, RAJASTHAN, GUJARAT, MADHYA PRADESH
1h		6th-7th& 14th CENTURY	GUJARAT, MADHYA PRADESH, UTTAR PRADESH, ASSAM, BIHAR, MAHARASHTRA, RAJASTHAN
1i		9th CENTURY	GUJARAT, MADHYA PRADESH, UTTAR PRADESH, ORISSA, ORISSA, BENGAL, RAJASTHAN, TAMIL NADU
1j	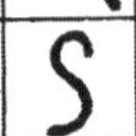	11th CENTURY	MAHARASHTRA, UTTAR PRADESH, BIHAR
1k	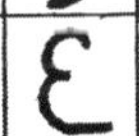	6th-7th-11th & 12th CENTURY	MAHARASHTRA, AFGHANISTAN MADHYA PRADESH, BIHAR,
1l		14th CENTURY	KARNATAKA
1m		12th CENTURY	MADHYA PRADESH
1n		10th CENTURY	MADHYA PRADESH, UTTAR PRADESH, ORISSA
1o		13th CENTURY	MADHYA PRADESH, RAJASTHAN
1p	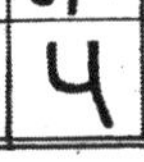	14th CENTURY	BIHAR

Fig. 5. Symbol for *Oṁ* or *Siddhaṁ*: Variant 1

PERIOD OF EMERGENCE			VARIANT 2
2		SECOND CENTURY	MATHURA
2a		THIRD CENTURY	ANDHRA PRADESH, MADHYA PRADESH GUJARAT
2b	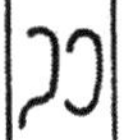	THIRD CENTURY	ANDHRA PRADESH, MADHYA PRADESH, ORISSA, MAHARASHTRA, RAJASTHAN, UTTAR PRADESH, NEPAL
2c		FOURTH CENTURY	ANDHRA PRADESH, BIHAR, GUJARAT, MADHYA PRADESH, KARNATAKA, JAMMU & KASHMIR, NEPAL
2d		FOURTH CENTURY	ORISSA, ANDHRA PRADESH, MADHYA PRADESH
2e		SEVENTH CENTURY	KARNATAKA. ANDHRA PRADESH, TAMIL NADU, ORISSA.
2f		TENTH CENTURY	KARNATAKA, MAHARASHTRA, ANDHRA PRADESH
2g		SIXTH CENTURY	BIHAR, ORISSA, RAJASTHAN, HIMACHAL PRADESH, MADHYA PRADESH, MAHARASHTRA
2h		SIXTH CENTURY	MADHYA PRADESH, MAHARASHTRA, RAJASTHAN, ORISSA, HIMACHAL PRADESH, GUJARAT
2i		SEVENTH CENTURY	EASTERN INDIA, AFGHANISTAN
2j		EIGHTH CENTURY	MAHARASHTRA, BIHAR, MADHYA PRADESH
2k		TENTH-ELEVENTH CENTURY	SOUTH INDIA
2ℓ		EIGHTH CENTURY	MADHYA PRADESH, MAHARASHTRA, KARNATAKA, BENGAL ORISSA, HIMACHAL PRADESH
2m		ELEVENTH CENTURY	KARNATAKA
2n		TENTH CENTURY	GUJARAT

Fig. 6. Symbol for *Oṁ* or *Siddhaṁ*: Variant 2

the word *siddhaṁ*.

Variant 1a: It occurs for the first time in the Nagarjunakonda inscription of the Ikshvāku king Ehuvala Chāṁtamūla, year 24 (*EI*, XXXV, p. 11). Here the symbol is preceded by the word *siddhaṁ*. But for the downward tail, the form bears close resemblance to its later variants. Yet the symbol has never been repeated in other Ikshvāku records. The inscription referred to above is datable to the last quarter of the third or the beginning of the fourth century.

Variant 1b: The earliest evidence of this stage of development comes from the Penukonda plates of Mādhava II (III) (*EI*, XIV, p. 331) ascribable to *circa* fifth century. During the seventh to the ninth centuries the form seems to have attained popularity in Andhra Pradesh, Madhya Pradesh and Orissa although it occurs sporadically in Assam as well as in Tamil Nadu.

Variant 1c: But for an upward turn it does not basically differ from the previous series. The form is met with as early as the fourth century in the Siroda plates of Devarāja (*EI*, XXIV, p. 143). It appears also in the Bhamodra Mohota plate of Droṇasiṁha, AD 502 (*EI*, XVI, p. 17), Palitana plates of Siṁhāditya and of Dhruvasena I (*EI*, II, p. 22) and in the grant of Śāntilla (*EI*, II, p. 21), thereby suggesting its popularity in the Gujarat region during the sixth century. However, that it was not confined to one locality is evident from its presence in the Barwani plate of Subandhu (AD 417) from Madhya Pradesh (*CII*, IV, pt. I, p. 17), Sarabhavaram plates of the Lord of Chikura from Rajahamundry, Andhra Pradesh (*EI*, XIII, p. 104) and the Nalanda seals of Harsha (*EI*, XXI, p. 74).

Variant 1d: In this case the form has already assumed a spiral character. As evident from one of the Kanheri records, it must have emerged sometime in the fourth-fifth centuries AD.[2] The Abhona plate of Śaṅkaragaṇa, datable to AD 597 (*CII*, IV, pt. 1, p. 38) provides the second landmark: the record belongs to the early Kalachuris. But this variety appears to have been mainly confined to Karnataka, Andhra Pradesh, Maharashtra and Madhya Pradesh between the eighth and the thirteenth centuries.

Variant 1e: It differs from the last-mentioned one in having more than one coil around the centre. Perhaps this shape was formed sometime in the beginning of the eighth century, when it appears in the Rayagad plates of Vijayāditya (*EI*, X, p. 14). In the period between the ninth and the fourteenth centuries it has been used in several epigraphs from Karnataka, Gujarat and Andhra Pradesh; it is frequently noticed along with other spiral forms in the records from District Dharwar, Karnataka.

Variant 1f: As indicated above, different varieties of the spiral became quite popular in the Karnataka area. In the last stage of its development it takes the shape of an ornate symbol. The period of its use would fall sometime in the eleventh century (*EI*, XVI, pp. 66 and 332; XII, p. 268, etc.). Figure 5 gives some of the commonly used forms of the ornate symbols.

Variant 1g: Variant 1f is the culmination of a line of development while Variant 1g marks the beginning of another. The descending tail of the latter is a feature which distinguishes it from Variant 1b. This is an oft-repeated form and is found in the inscriptions from Orissa, Bengal, Gujarat, Madhya Pradesh, Rajasthan, Maharashtra and Andhra Pradesh: it has the highest incidence in the records from Orissa where it occurs between the seventh and the fourteenth century.

Variant 1h: In this case the symbol takes more or less a vertical appearance, and occurs for the first time in the Ghugrahati copper-plate inscription of Samāchāra-deva, ascribable to the sixth century (*EI*, XVIII, p. 74). It is a fairly widespread form and is noticed in the records from Madhya Pradesh, Bihar, Assam, Maharashtra, Orissa, Uttar Pradesh, Gujarat, Bengal and Rajasthan, ranging in date from the seventh to the fourteenth-fifteenth centuries (pl. IV B).

Variant 1i: It is very similar to the previous one but seems to be a later introduction, for it occurs for the first time in the Karitalai stone inscription of Lakshmaṇarāja I, AD 840-41 (*CII*, IV pt. 1, p. 178). The use of this variant can be seen in the inscriptions from Assam, Gujarat, Maharashtra, Tamil Nadu, Madhya Pradesh, Rajasthan, Uttar Pradesh and Orissa. On the whole, the geographical distribution of Variants 1h and 1i covers a far larger area than any of the forms mentioned above.

Variant 1j: The form occurs in some records, of the eleventh and twelfth centuries, from Bombay, Banaras and Monghyr.

Variant 1k: It has been occasionally used in the inscriptions of the eleventh and twelfth centuries although it dates back of the Kabul inscriptions of Shāhī Khiṁgāla (*EI*, XXXV, p. 44). But its main sphere of distribution seems to be Madhya Pradesh, Maharashtra and the Bodh-Gaya region in Bihar.

Variant 1l: It is noticed in the Kalyana inscription of Sultān Muḥammad, Śaka 1248, from Karnataka (*EI*, XXXII, p. 165).

Variant 1m: This form has been used quite often in the Chandella inscriptions of the twelfth-thirteenth centuries. The Tewar stone-inscription of Jayasiṁha, AD 1177 (*CII*, IV, pt. 1, p. 344) and the two inscriptions of the time of Gopāla, AD 1283 (*EI*, XXXIII, p. 31) have symbols almost similar to the present one. Perhaps the form was characteristic of a certain group of records from central India.

Variant 1n: The Ghumli plates of Bashkaladeva, AD 989 (*EI*, XXXI,

p. 11) offer the earliest example of this form. Noticed generally in the records of central India, it has been used also in Gāhaḍavāla records from Uttar Pradesh (*EI*, XXXV, p. 201).

Variant 1o: This form seems to be a further development of Variant 1n and is found in a Jaina record from Mount Abu in Rajasthan (*EI*, VIII, p. 219). It occurs quite frequently in the Jaina manuscripts of the twelfth-thirteenth centuries.[3]

Variant 2: The original prototype (figs. 6, 7). The earliest example of this form comes from the Kushāṇa records of the (Śaka) year 41 (AD 119) of Huvishka's time from Mathura (*EI*, X, p. 114: XXI, p. 55). D.C. Sircar describes it as "resembling an Aśokan ṭā with the opening to left".[4] Generally, it occupies a position only next to the word *siddhaṁ*.

Variant 2a: The horizontal stroke noticed in the previous form is absent in this case. Looking like an arc, it appears for the first time in an inscription of the time of Ehuvala Chāṁtamūla, year 16, from Nagarjunakonda (*EI*, XXXIV, p. 17). Here, too, the symbol follows the word *siddhaṁ*; a double *daṇḍa* intervenes in between the symbol and the opening formula. The Betul plates of Saṁkshobha, AD 518 (*EI*, VIII, p. 284) and the Brahmanapalli grant of Karkka Suvarṇṇavarsha, AD 824 (*EI*, XXII, p. 84) also contain identical mark.

Variant 2b: Dating back to about the second half of the third century, it has been noticed in several records from a wide geographical area. Chronologically, it should be placed earlier than Variant 2a, for Variant 2b occurs for the first time in the Uppugundur inscription of the Ikshvāku king Vīrapurushadatta (*EI*, XXXIII, p. 189) who was the predecessor of Ehuvala Chāṁtamūla, mentioned above. In the Ikshvāku records from Nagarjunakonda and Uppugundur are to be seen three different forms of this symbol; the one included under Variant 1a is chronologically later than the other two.

This very form occurs in two epigraphs of the Gupta period from Kathiawar; they are dated to the fourth century. In the fifth century, the symbol takes the shape similar to Bengali alphabet *ta* or Hindi numeral for seven, and is used in the Vilavatti grant of Pallava Siṁhavarman (*EI*, XXIV, p. 296) from Andhra Pradesh and in the Karitalai copper-plate inscriptions of Mahārāja Jayanātha, from district Jabalpur (*CII*, III, p. 117). In the former, the symbol marks the end of the record. Its appearance in an inscription from Nepal goes back to as early as the fifth century.[5] The popularity of this form attained height during the sixth and seventh centuries when it is found in several inscriptions from Gujarat, Madhya Pradesh, Orissa, Andhra Pradesh, Maharashtra, Rajasthan and Uttar Pradesh. It becomes rare after the seventh century although it continues to be used till about the fifteenth century; the Peshawar Museum inscription of Vāṇhaḍaka (*EI*, X, p. 79) includes one of its latest example.

Variant 2c: This variety is found in several inscriptions of the Sālaṅkāyana kings from Andhra Pradesh. Some of these inscriptions have been ascribed to the fourth century (*EI*, IX, p. 56; XXXI, p. 1). Also, it is noticed in the Nalanda spurious plate of Samudragupta, of the year 5 (*EI*, XXV, p. 50). Thus the period of its development may easily be placed in the fourth century. During the fifth-sixth centuries the form remained confined to Andhra Pradesh and Maharashtra. In the seventh century it spread to other parts like Gujarat, Bihar, Nepal, Madhya Pradesh, Karnataka, Rajasthan and Kashmir. Thus its geographical horizon is almost coterminous with that of the Variant 2b. The Alupa inscriptions at Udiyavara (*EI*, IX, p. 15) ranging in date from the seventh to the eleventh centuries show the use of this form in the Karnataka region even after the eighth century; it is reported occasionally from other regions like Maharashtra, Andhra Pradesh and Orissa.

Variant 2d: The variety, a spiral design, is noticed in the fourth century in the Penugonda plates of Hastivarman, a Sālaṅkāyana king (*EI*, XXXV, p. 145). Frequently used during the fifth century in inscriptions from Orissa, Andhra Pradesh, Madhya Pradesh and Maharashtra, it becomes popular in the Karnataka region from the sixth to the tenth centuries. It occurs in the inscriptions of the sixth and seventh centuries discovered from Andhra Pradesh, Orissa, Maharashtra and Madhya Pradesh. Significantly, it is rare or non-existent in the epigraphs found from north India.

Variant 2e: The form is a developed spiral and came into being sometime in the seventh century in Orissa and the Karnataka region as is evident from Patiakella grant of Mahārāja Śivarāja (*EI*, IX, p. 285) and the Aihole inscription of Pulikeśin II (*EI*, VI, p.1). It occurs twice in the latter inscription: the main epigraph as well as the subsequent addition to it conclude with this very symbol. Outside Karnataka it is noticed in a few inscriptions from Andhra Pradesh, Tamil Nadu and Orissa.

Variant 2f: The ornate spiral appears for the first time in the Kadalur grant of Narasiṁha II (*EI*, XXXVI, p. 97) in AD 962. Confined mainly to the Karnataka region, it has been used very sporadically in Maharashtra and Andhra Pradesh.

Variant 2g: Found in several inscriptions from Bihar, Orissa, Rajasthan, Madhya Pradesh and Maharashtra, it has been used as early as the sixth century in the Nalanda stone inscription of the reign of Yaśovarmmadeva (*EI*, XX, p. 37). It became popular in the seventh-eighth centuries. A peculiar development of this form is noticed in the inscriptions from Chamba.[6]

Variant 2h: Four copper-plates from Soro (*EI*, XXIII, p. 197), district

DIFFERENT VARIETIES OF THE
VARIANT 2 (WITH ARM

SUB - VARIETY	2	2a	2b	2c	2d	2e	

PERIOD OF EMERGENCE	2nd CENTURY	3rd CENTURY	3rd CENTURY	5th CENTURY	6th CENTURY	7th CENTURY	C
AREA OF CONCENTRATION	MATHURA	NAGAR JUNA - - KONDA-	UPPUG- -UNDUR				R K
NO.OF SPECIMENS	1	1	1	47	13	7	

Fig. 7. Different varieties of the symbol for *Oṁ* o

YMBOL FOR SIDDHAM OR OM
URNED TO THE LEFT)

			7th CENTURY	11th CENTURY				
NDHRA RISSA, ADHYA ADESH AHA- ASHTRA ASTHAN JARAT NATAKA	KARN- -ATAKA	EASTERN INDIA TO THE EAST OF KANPUR	SANJAN SHAHA- -BAD CHANDA	SOUTH INDIA	SOUTH INDIA	SAGAR NANDER BELGAUM FARIDPUR RAIPUR SONEPUR STATE	KARN- -ATAKA	GUJARAT
h TO 10th ENTURY	10th TO 11th CENTURY	11th TO 13th CENTURY	7th TO 8th CENTURY			10th TO 15th CENTURY	11th CENTURY	11th CENTURY.
47	4	26	3	3	3	6	3	1

r *Siddhaṁ*: Variant 2 (with arm turned to the left)

Balasore, datable to the first half of the sixth century contain this form of the symbol which has been used during the seventh to the ninth century in Madhya Pradesh, Gujarat, Maharashtra, Orissa, Rajasthan and Chamba in Himachal Pradesh.

Variant 2i: Significantly, the form is peculiar to eastern India[7] during the seventh to the thirteenth century; it is rarely found outside this region. The Mankuwar stone image inscription of Kumāragupta, AD 448, reveals its earliest example. A form very similar to this variant is to be seen in a Śāradā inscription from Hund, near Kabul, dated to AD 774-75 (*EI*, XXII, p. 97).

Variant 2j: The Sanjan plates of Buddhavarsha (*EI*, XIV, p. 144), the Mangraon inscription of Vishṇugupta's time from district Shahabad (*EI*, XXVI, p. 241), and the Bhandak plates of Krishṇarāja I, AD 772, from district Chanda (*EI*, XIV p. 121) contain this variety which seems quite similar to either Variant 2b or 2g.

Variant 2k: Known in the south India as *piḷḷaiyar sūḷi*, it makes its appearance there in the tenth-eleventh centuries and is absent in north India. The Pehoa inscription of the reign of Mahendrapāla contains a symbol very similar to this form (*EI*, I, p. 242-250).

Variant 2l: The variant looks like letter O of the modern Bengali alphabet although its earliest example comes from an eighth century epigraph—the Saugor (Sagar) stone inscription of Śaṅkaragaṇa (*EI*, XXVII, p. 163) from district Sagar. It, however, occurs in the Madanapada plate of Viśvarūpasena (*EI*, XXXIII, p. 315) from Faridpur, East Bengal (now Bangladesh)and is datable to the twelfth-thirteenth centuries. During the tenth century the form is noticed in some inscriptions from Maharashtra and Karnataka. Some records of the Chamba region ascribable to the eleventh-twelfth centuries have the form inscribed.[8] It occurs also in the Pendrabandh plates of Pratāpamalla, AD 1213, from Raipur (*EI*, XXIII, p. 1); the Mahada plates of Yogeśvaradevavarman from Orissa, dated to AD 1508 (*EI*, XII, p. 218) is the latest known example.

Variant 2m: Only a few epigraphs of the eleventh century, all of them from district Dharwar, Karnataka, have made use of the form, which looks like the letter *e* of the modern Bengali alphabet.

Variant 2n: Represented by a solitary example, it occurs in the Ghumli plates of Bashkaladeva, AD 989, from Saurashtra (*EI*, XXXI, p. 11).

2. General Observations

As already stated, the symbol under study shows a widespread distribution. Yet there are areas where its incidence is extremely high. It will be evident from fig. 8 that Madhya Pradesh has yielded the maximum number of 21

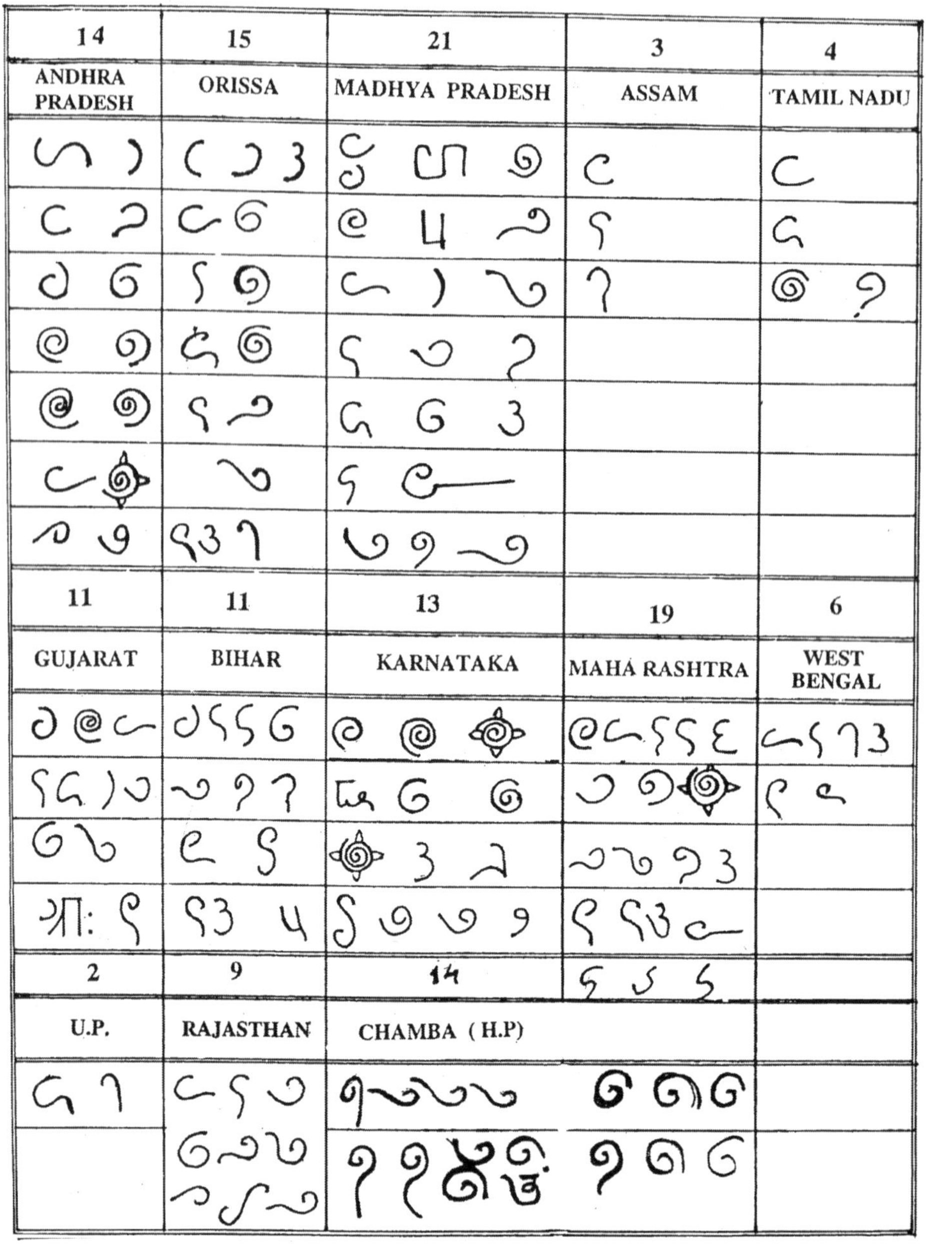

Fig. 8. Symbol for *Oṁ* or *Siddhaṁ*: distribution and relative incidence

varieties, whereas Andhra Pradesh, Orissa, Maharashtra, Gujarat and Karnataka have produced 11 to 15 variants. The area comprising Andhra Pradesh, Orissa, Madhya Pradesh, Maharashtra, Gujarat and Karnataka thus constitutes the area of high incidence. Rajasthan, Bengal, Tamil Nadu, Assam, Uttar Pradesh and Himachal Pradesh where only 3 to 6 varieties are found form the area of low incidence. There is a third zone, consisting of western Uttar Pradesh, Punjab and Sind, which has hardly revealed any form in the period of mature development of this symbol. It may be recalled here that many of the variants made their first appearance in the area of high incidence.

Yet, so far as the present knowledge goes, both the variants, or their prototypes, occur for the first time in the Kushāṇa records from Mathura; and both of them cannot be connected with certainty with any known symbol of the pre-Kushāṇa times. These may, however, be considered a modified triskelion, the earliest representation of which is found in the Erragudi and Rajula-Mandagiri Minor Rock-Edicts of Aśoka, both the places falling within the zone of high incidence. Anyway, from Mathura both the forms spread to Andhra Pradesh where they appear in some Ikshvāku and Sālaṅkāyana records.

In meaning and significance, the *vāma-āvarta* and the *dakṣhina-āvarta* varieties do not differ from each other as they occur side by side in the records of the same locality or dynasty. Thus in the Kushāṇa and Ikshvāku inscriptions both the types occur almost at the same time. The Palitana plates of the Maitraka ruler Dhruvasena I (*EI*, XI, p. 104) offer a very convincing proof. Three inscriptions of the king ranging in date from AD 526 to 529, all of them engraved by one Kikkaka, contain two different variants belonging to the *vāma-āvarta* and *dakshiṇa-āvarta* types. Similarly, both the variants are to be seen used together in the Penukonda plates of Mādhava II (*EI*, XIV, p. 331). Six Saindhava copper-plates from Ghumli (*EI*, XXVI, p. 185), Indian Museum plates of Gaṅga Indravarman (*EI*, XXVI, p. 165), etc., also show the use of both the varieties side by side even in the same record. Examples may be multiplied to show that the direction of the symbol has no bearing on its meaning and significance.

It is not known if the variations of forms are accompanied by new or changed meaning and connotation, and despite such marked evolution, the symbol retains a degree of its fundamental attributes. For instance, even in particular areas, e.g., Chamba in Himachal Pradesh (fig. 9) or in areas under the influence of specific dynasties such as the Vākāṭakas and Kalachuris (fig. 10) the symbol with its variety of forms occurs, while retaining its original meaning.[9] A few attempts that have been made to interpret the symbol aim more or less in ascribing a common meaning

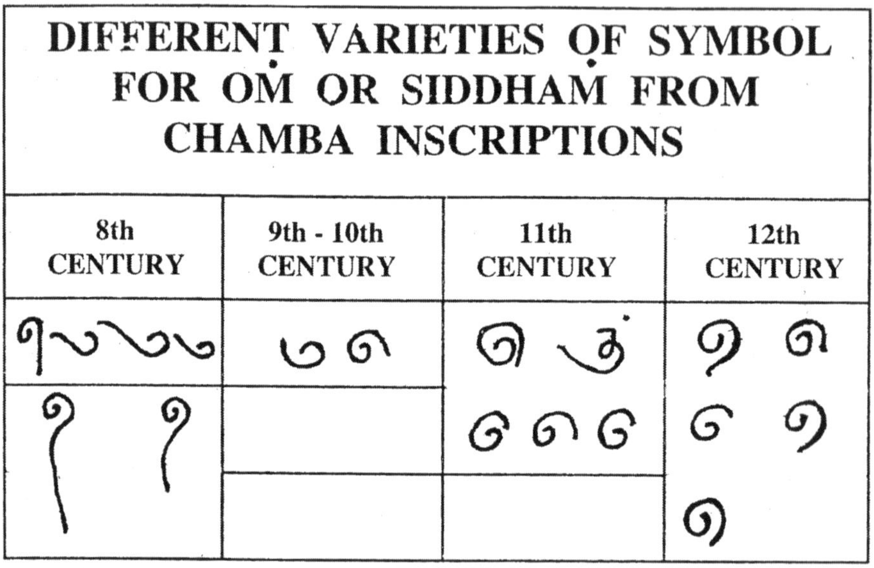

Fig. 9. Different varieties of symbol for *Oṁ* or *Siddhaṁ* from Chamba inscriptions

throughout. Everyone, however, agrees to consider it as an auspicious mark.[10] Eminent epigraphists like Hoernle and Fleet have taken the symbol as indicating *praṇava* or the sacred syllable *Oṁ*.[11] Even Al-Birūni has described the form as expressing the sound *Oṁ*. The earlier epigraphists perhaps based their readings largely on the interpretation of Al-Birūni. This view continued to hold the ground till 1923-24 when Nalinikanta Bhattasali challenged the theory (*EI*, XVII, p. 349). Bhattasali's view was also accepted by the then editor of the *Epigraphia Indica,* H. Krishna Sastri, and both of them held that the symbol stands for *siddhaṁ*; the later epigraphists have generally taken the symbol as representing *siddhaṁ,* and not as *Oṁ*.

According to D.C. Sircar, "the symbol stood for the word *siddhaṁ* found at the beginning of numerous early inscriptions. But there is evidence to show that sometimes the symbol was pronounced as *Oṁ siddhiḥ* and Al-Birūni seems to have confused this *Oṁ siddhiḥ* with *Oṁ*".[12] He has also cited instances of such confusion in Indian epigraphs. Unfortunately, the evolutionary aspect of the symbol has largely escaped notice of the scholars. Likewise, the possibility of the meaning of the symbol getting transformed with the changing time and circumstances is also not taken into account.

It may be mentioned here that the symbol depicted by Al-Birūni corresponds to Variant 2k of the present classification. This form is confined largely to south India and hardly occurs in any inscription from the north.

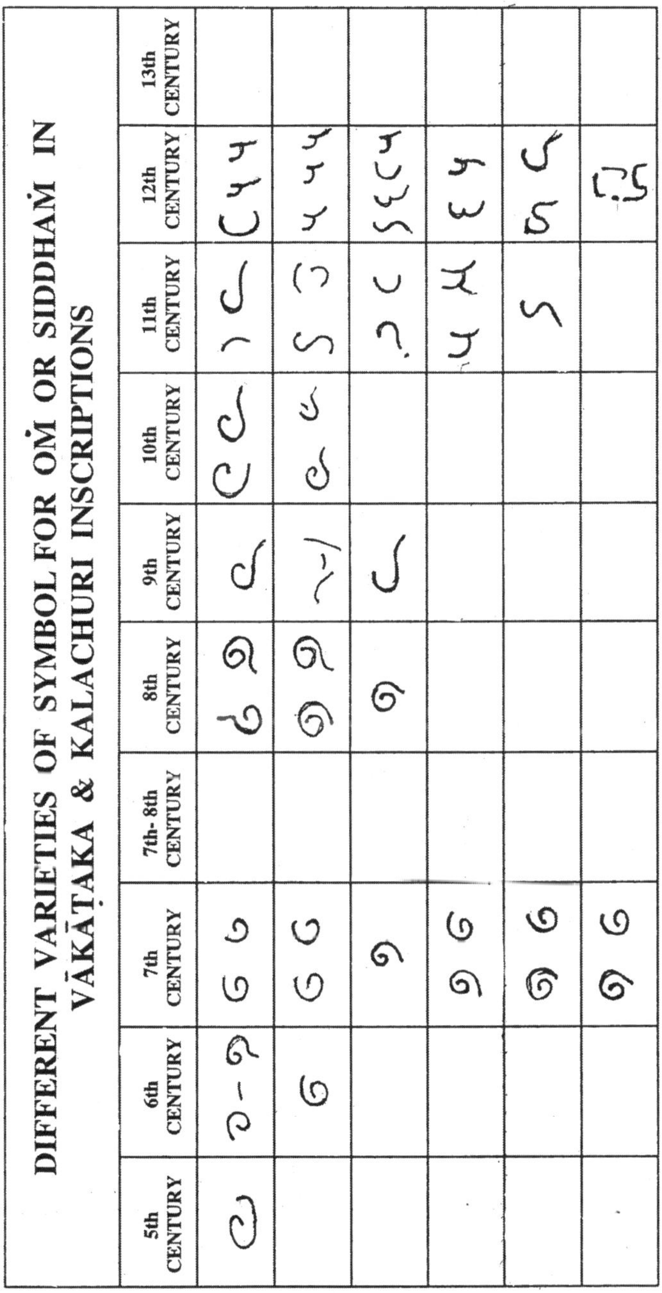

Fig. 10. Different varieties of symbol for *Oṁ* or *Siddhaṁ* in Vākāṭaka and Kalachuri inscriptions

Similarly, the form that Bhattasali has taken into account corresponds to Variants 1h and 2j dating back respectively to the sixth and eighth centuries. Bhattasali writes: "In Bengal, this symbol was largely used in all ancient documents and manuscripts and in teaching alphabets to beginners they were taught to draw this symbol to start with. This custom was prevalent as late as twenty-five years ago, but has disappeared by this time. This symbol was called *aṁji* and was supposed to signify the god Gaṇeśa, the giver of success, being drawn to represent his elephant's trunk. In reading, it was read *Siddhirastu*".[12] Variant 2k, in Tamil region, is also known as *Piḷḷaiyar sūḻi* for Gaṇeśa's curl which is first taught to be drawn by children before they start learning alphabets. In the circumstances, one has to accept the fact that at one time or the other in the history of the symbol a later form got associated with Gaṇeśa's curl at least in certain regions of India. But certainly it was not a universally-accepted meaning, for, in the Telugu areas the form similar to Variant 1d of the present classification is still in vogue and the symbol stands for *Śrī*. The orthodox practice is to commence any writing with the letter *Śrī* or a symbol representing it (*EI*, XVIII, p. 346). This form dates back to about the fourth-fifth centuries AD and is confined to the area of high incidence. There is, then, evidence to show that the symbol acquired two different meanings—*Siddhaṁ* and *Śrī*—in different regions, perhaps in two different temporal contexts.

Mention may be made of the fact that inscriptions open also with the expression *Śrī*. It is characteristic generally of the south where several Chola inscriptions begin with *Śrī svasti* or *svasti Śrī* (*EI*, VI, pp. 20, 278; VIII, pp. 1 and 260). Further, the word *Śrī* has been engraved in the upper margin of the first plate in the Rajapura plates of Madhurāntakadeva, Śaka 987, from Bastar (*EI*, IX, p. 174). Again, the Yenamadala inscription of Gaṇapāṁbā, AD 1249 (*EI*, III, p. 94) begins with *Śrī Śrī*. The use of *Śrī* is, however, not unknown in the north as it occurs in the Lucknow Museum plate of Kīrtipāla, AD 1111 (*EI*, VII, p. 93). All this may indicate that *Śrī,* like *siddhaṁ*, or *śubhamastu, svasti* and *Oṁ* in the preamble of the inscription has been used as an auspicious invocation in some regions. And the present day usage in the Andhra Pradesh shows that *Śrī* too is expressed by a symbol very similar to one of the forms presented here. As a corollary, it may be also said that the same symbol has been used in some areas as *Śrī* and at other places as *siddhaṁ,* at least in some period of its development. Now, D.C. Sircar has already shown that "the symbol was pronounced as *Oṁ siddhiḥ*". Obviously, different meanings were given to the same group of symbols in different times and regions, although its original connotation is still unknown.[14]

One of the arguments of Bhattasali in discarding the equation of the symbol with *Oṁ* is that "in some inscriptions the symbol is found to precede *Oṁ*, which would never have been the case if the two were identical". The same argument holds good in case of the occurrence of the symbol with the expression *siddhaṁ*. D.C. Sircar, while editing the inscription of Ehuvala Chāṁtamūla, year 24 (*EI*, XXXV, p. 11) has, however, tried to explain the presence of the symbol after the word *siddhaṁ* as due to scribe's inadvertence. But this is not a solitary example, for all the Ikshvāku inscriptions where the symbol appears, have followed the same pattern (*EI*, XXXIII, p. 189; XXXIV, p. 9 and XXXV, p. 11). In some Mathura inscriptions of Huvishka (*EI*, X, p. 112 ff; XXI, p. 55) also the symbol is preceded by the opening formula *siddhaṁ*. Evidently, so many cases can hardly be explained as scribal error.

Siddhaṁ as a preamble of the inscription starts with the Kushāṇa records of Kanishka's time. No record of Aśoka's time opens with *siddhaṁ* or any other equivalent *svasti-vachana*, expressed either in words or in symbols. Even the inscriptions of the Indo-Greek and Śuṅga rulers do not have any auspicious word like *siddhaṁ* or the salutation to the protective deity. It seems that the practice of salutation to the presiding deity started before the use of the expression *siddhaṁ*, for *Namo Arahantānaṁ* and *Nama arahato Vardhamānasa* occur respectively in the Hathigumpha cave inscription of Khāravela (first century BC) and the Mathura votive tablet of the time of Soḍāsa (first quarter of the first century). During this period and even earlier, several auspicious symbols like *svastika*, standard-within-railing, etc., appear in the inscriptions. In fact, the marks occuring in Kanishka's or Huvishka's record are amongst the latest arrivals. It seems, therefore, quite unlikely that the symbol was intended to substitute the expression *siddhaṁ*, which itself was a new introduction at that time. Thus, the original significance of this symbol is not easy to determine.

Its original form, unless it is a triskelion, is also not easy to comprehend. Two different types occur in the Kushāṇa records while the Ikshvāku inscriptions of the third century contain as many as four varieties. It seems, therefore, that the symbol even by the third century did not assume a definite form, which might have taken place in the fourth century. Some varieties of the symbol, specially Variant 2a of the present classification may, however, be compared with those of the Kalsi edict of Aśoka. But it is not known whether these marks at the end of several edicts at Kalsi are symbols or marks of interpunctuation.[15]

Whatever may be the original form and meaning of the symbol under study, it underwent gradual transformation in different areas, and with the change of form it acquired new meaning and significance. As already pointed out, the symbol might have been regarded variously as *siddhaṁ*, *Śrī* and

Oṁ[16] in different stages of its development. Some scholars have taken its spiral variety as a conventional representation of *śaṅkha*. But it has been shown that spirals of this symbol is the culmination of a line of development, and hence, the spirals of this symbol have to be distinguished from real ones with their antiquity stretching back to the palaeolithic times; such spirals do not occur in the inscriptions as well.

One cannot, however, rule out the possibility of the spiral variety of this symbol acquiring at a later date certain elements connected with the magico-religious motif of true spirals. As shown in Chapter 6 *śaṅkha* is a favourite motif in Indian inscriptions, and generally the full or the side view of the conches are depicted there. On the other hand, spirals, as several authorities think, were the outcome of magico-religious use of the whorled shell. In the last analysis, it is an imitative symbol—imitations of several natural objects and phenomena. According to Mackenzie: "It is found in nature as we have seen, for certain climbing plants ascend supports in spiral shape, certain shells are of spiral shape and there are waterspouts, whirlwinds and whirlpools".[17] But in course of time the symbol must have assumed various meanings in different periods and in different social or cultural setup;[18] various ideas and philosophical interpretations[19] sprang forth centering the symbol. Some such high concept might have got mixed up with the spiral variety of the auspicious symbol used in the opening of the inscriptions.

The ornate spirals so common in the Karnataka region reflect their fusion with the idea associated with the floral design, which indeed, is another oft-repeated auspicious mark in Indian inscriptions. Evidently, the spirals of the Karnataka region imbibed some composite character: in certain cases the concept of spiral derived from whorled-shell got merged with the symbol, while in other cases the floral motif combined with the spiral presented complex form symbolizing a blend of several ideas associated with *maṅgala*.

Notes and References

1. Ahmad Hasan Dani in his *Indian Palaeography* (Oxford, 1963), p. 21, writes about the "auspicious sound *oṁ*" which "in North India . . . generally assumes the form of a curled head with a tail either to the left, right or bottom. In South India this tail is generally spiral". But it will be evident from the following pages that the pattern of development of the auspicious symbol is not so simple as envisaged by Dani. His regional classification is also not based on sufficient data, and hence is not valid. Also see the work mentioned below (f. n. 3) where an attempt is made to present an evolutionary sequence

of the auspicious symbol. Also see, Gaurishankar Hirachand Ojha, *Bhāratīya Prāchīna Lipimālā* (in Hindi) (Ajmer, V.S. 1975), pp. 148-149.

2. Jas. Burgess, *Report on the Elura Cave Temples and the Brahmanical and Jaina Caves in Western India,* Archaeological Survey of Western India, Vol. V (London, 1883), p. 77.
3. Sarabhai Manilal Nawab, *Jaina Chitrakalpadruma* (in Gujarati) (Ahmedabad, 1936), pp. 57-61.
4. Dines Chandra Sircar, *Select Inscriptions bearing on Indian History and Civilization* (Calcutta, 1965), I, p. 156n.
5. Pandit Bhagvanlal Indraji, *Twenty-three Inscriptions from Nepal* (Bombay, 1885).
6. J. Ph. Vögel, *Antiquities of Chamba State*, Archaeological Survey of India, New Imperial Series, XXXVI, pt. I (Calcutta, 1911), pp. 142-45.
7. D.C. Sircar writes: "the symbol was generally used till modern times in the eastern areas with the sign of nasalisation placed above the Bengali figure for 7 or as the figure 4 as found in medieval inscriptions from Bengal." See his *Indian Epigraphy* (Delhi, 1965), p. 93.
8. J. Ph. Vögel, *op.cit.*, p. 159.
9. Analysis of this symbol occurring in inscriptions in terms of specific dynasties, or in terms of specific area or period is likely to provide interesting results. This, however, has not been attempted by us in the present study.
10. D.C. Sircar, *Ind. Epi., op.cit.* (1965), p. 92. He writes: "A *maṅgala* i.e. a benediction or an auspicious word, at the beginning, in the middle and at the end of a composition, was believed to ensure its completion and preservation". He has also made an attempt to show how "the symbol was gradually modified" in course of time.
11. For full discussion, see Nalinikanta Bhattasali, 'Some image inscriptions from East Bengal', *EI*, XVII (1923-24), pp. 349-62.
12. D.C. Sircar, *Ind. Epi. op.cit.* (1965), p. 93.
13. Nalinikanta Bhattasali, *op.cit.*, p. 352.
14. In Marwar, the auspicious symbol taught to the children at the time of initiation in studies is known as *Be liti, Bhale, Mindu, and Bepaṇ* which stand for auspicious cipher looking like Hindi numeral 50 followed by *Oṁ namaḥ*. The symbol is similar to Variant 1*n* of the present classification. See, Nawab, *op.cit.*, p. 58.
15. D.C. Sircar, *Ind. Epi., op.cit.* (1965), p. 95.
16. In modern times *Oṁ* in different parts of north India is written like an alphabet similar to variant 2*l* with a nasal mark.
17. Donald A. Mackenzie, *The Migration of Symbols* (London, 1926), p. 66.
18. G. Eliot Smith in his *Elephants and Ethnologists* (London and New York, 1924) writes (p. 90): "Many facts played a part in the development of spiral symbolism and in bringing about its intimate association with the elephant". He further states: "Throughout a wide area of the Old World the spiral ornament is a distinctive symbol of thunder and of the god of thunder".
19. Take for instance the concept of *Kuṇḍalinī*, the coiled serpent—a spiral.

CHAPTER 5

FLORAL, ORNAMENTAL AND VEGETAL SYMBOLS

In Indian tradition the flower is a *maṅgala*; it is a must in Brahmanical religious ceremonies. Of all the flowers, lotus is the most sacred and has, in India, a hoary past. It is conceived even as a personified deity—Padmapurusha.[1] It is associated with or is an inseparable attribute of some Buddhist gods and goddesses like Avalokiteśvara Padmapāṇi and Tārā. No wonder, therefore, that *padma*, or lotus would find its way also into the domain of auspicious symbols, and would make its appearance in the inscriptions too.

Many scholars have identified the floral and ornamental designs in the inscriptions as lotus although there is hardly any naturalistic representation of it in the inscriptions. They are more or less abstract pictures of some flower—flower as an auspicious mark. Some representations in epigraphical records do simulate floral forms while others tend largely towards geometrical—these symbols may have been intended to substitute flowers symbolizing good luck. There are also instances of the organic form being fused with geometrical ones.

Flowers depicted on ancient Indian coins also hardly show any naturalistic form; they are mostly idealized flowers. Some of them bear similarities with those appearing in the inscriptions. It is proposed to discuss this aspect after a brief survey of the floral and ornamental symbols appearing in the epigraphs. The Indian tradition also recognizes corn-inflorences or *mañjarī* and plant leaves—especially the sprouting leaves—as auspicious symbols. A few instances that occur in the inscriptions have also been dealt with in this chapter.

1. Floral design

As far as the present knowledge goes, the Basim plates of Vākāṭaka Vindhyaśakti II (*EI*, XXVI, p. 137), AD 400, contain the earliest example of flower (fig. 11, *1*) in an inscription. It is a four-petalled flower placed in between the two sets of *daṇḍa* or punctuation-mark at the end of the record. Two grants of Pravarasena II (*EI*, XXIV, p. 260) of the same Vākāṭaka family have at their end a flower with thirteen petals arranged round a circle representing the thalamus (fig. 11, *2*). All the records mentioned above come either from Akola or Wardha in Maharashtra forming part of the Vākāṭaka territory. There are a few more early records too depicting floral symbol at the end. Thus the Andhavaram plates of Ananta-śaktivarman datable to the fifth century (*EI*, XXVIII, p. 175) show a floral design between the two sets of triple *daṇḍas* followed by a wavy line at the end of the epigraph (fig. 11 *3*), which was discovered from district Srikakulam, Andhra Pradesh. The Kabul inscription of Shāhī Khiṅgala ascribable to the sixth-seventh centuries has also at the end a floral symbol (fig. 11, *4*) (*EI*, XXXV, p. 44). Thus, all the early examples of flower are to be seen only at the conclusion of the text, and not at the opening.

Despite its early occurrence, the symbol became popular in the inscriptions only during the medieval times, that too mostly in the Andhra Pradesh area. Inscriptions of the Eastern Chālukyas, Eastern Gaṅgas, Reḍḍis, etc., belonging to the tenth to the thirteenth centuries from Andhra Pradesh have this symbol incised either at the opening or the end, or at both the places of the same epigraph. It, however, seems that the practice of engraving floral symbols spread to Maharashtra quite early as is evident from the Talegaon copper-plates of Krishṇa-Rāja, I, AD 768. At the end of this Rāshṭrakūṭa record are to be seen two double circles each surrounding a floral design with five petals (fig. 11, *5*) (*EI*, XIII, p. 275). A Rāshṭrakūṭa record of AD 930 from Cambay (*EI*, VII, p. 26), of Govinda IV, has this symbol engraved at the end of line 67 (fig. 11, *6*) preceded by an expression *maṅgala mahāśrī*. The form of the symbol seems to have visual appeal as the floral members arranged on the thalamus comprise eight petals, four sepals and four bracts, the last-mentioned item being represented by shooting lines.

As already stated, the earliest example of a flower in an Andhra Pradesh record comes from the Andhavaram plates of Anantaśaktivarman (*EI*, XXVIII, p. 175) dated to the fifth century AD. A realistic representation of an eight-petalled flower with a curved stalk (fig. 11, *7*) is engraved on the Chidivalasa plates of Devendravarman, Gaṅga year 397, AD 893-95.[2] It is one of the finest examples in the collection of floral symbols in inscriptions. But the portrayal of lotus flowers with buds and leaves in a Nepalese inscription puts into shade all other examples. Carved above the inscriptions in bold lines, it depicts the scene of a lotus pond and bears testimony of a mature plastic tradition.

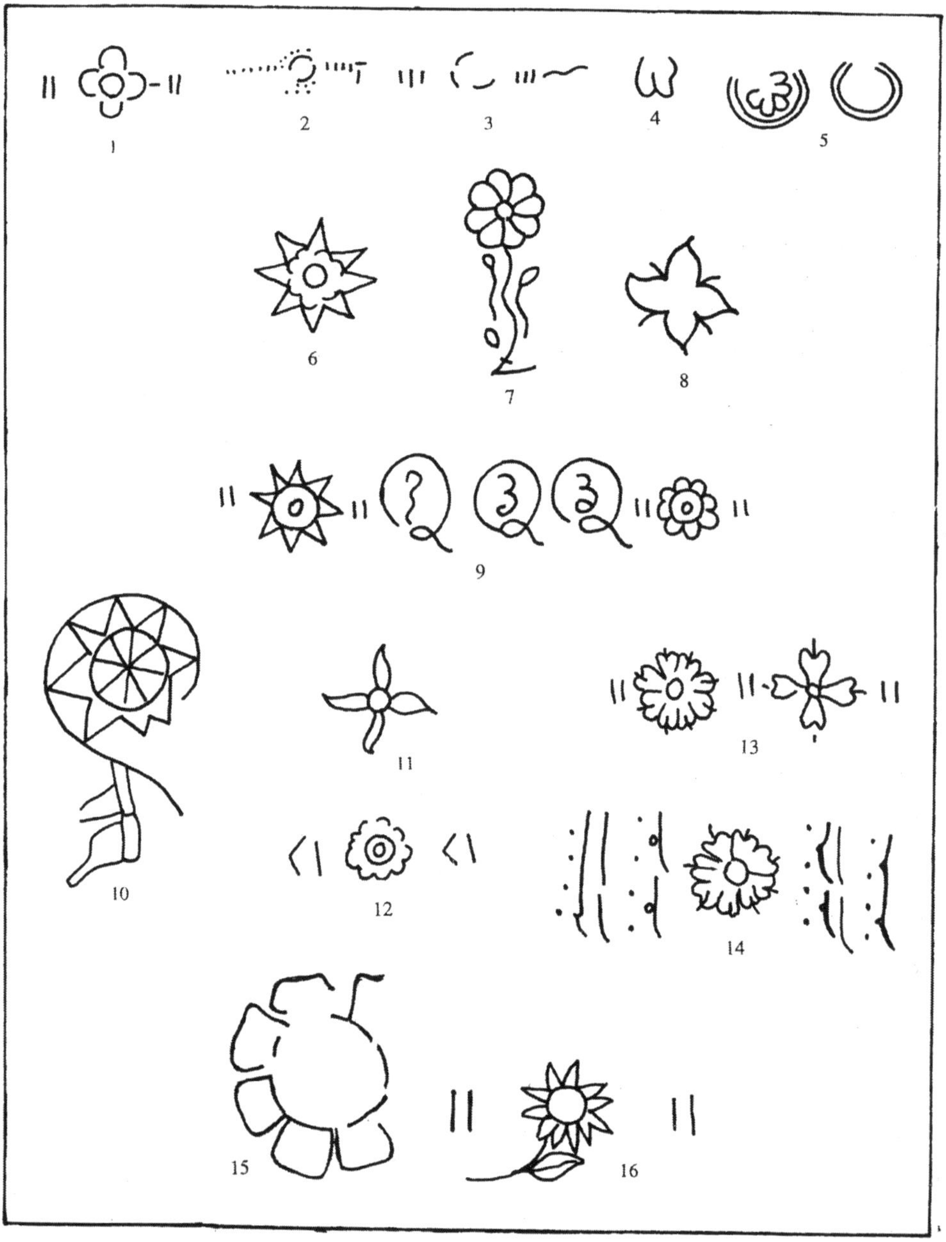

Fig. 11

The floral symbol could gain ground in Āndhradeśa only at the beginning of the tenth century, when it appears in several Eastern Chālukyan records. The symbols are now used at the opening, and some authorities take them as expressing the word *siddhaṁ*. In certain cases, the floral design is drawn not only at the beginning but also at the end. In the Masulipatam (?) plates of Chālukya Bhīma II, AD 934-945 (*EI*, V, p. 134) the flower (fig. 11, *8*) at the opening is followed by the word *svasti*; it is an example of a flower with four petals. But the Nandamapundi grant of Rājarāja I, AD 1053 (*EI*, IV, 300) starts with a flower, and also ends with it. A seven-petalled flower occurs at the beginning of the Kalidindi grant of the Eastern Chālukyan ruler Rājarāja I (*EI*, XXIX, p. 57). The floral design that is noticed at the end of the Chebrolu inscription of Jaya (*EI*, V, p. 142), AD 1213-14, is fully round a circle with a central pellet. Significantly, the inscription starts with *Svasti Srīḥ* and ends with *śrī śrī śrī* flanked on either side by a floral symbol (fig. 11, *9*). A similar design of a flower with eight triangular petals arranged around a thalamus also divided into eight segments (fig. 11, *10*), is noticed in the Pillalamari inscription of the reign of Kāpaya Nāyaka, Śaka 1279.[3] It seems to have a curled stalk with a solitary leaf drawn rather realistically. The Pentapadu grant of Choḍa Bhaktirāja, Śaka 1265 (*EI*, XXXIII, p. 219) begins with a simple four-petalled flower (fig. 11, *11*); its ninth plate contains the figure of the mythical bird *Gaṇḍabheruṇḍa* (see below, Chapter 8, fig. 18, *3*). Sometimes an inscription opens with a single mark, while two flowers are shown at the end as in the Pithapuran plates of Vīra-Choḍa (*EI*, V, p. 70). One of the latest known examples of a floral design comes from the Konkunduru plates, AD 1431, of Allaya-Doḍḍa, of the Reḍḍis of Koṇḍaviḍu (*EI*, V, p. 53). Here also the inscription starts with a conventional representation of a flower and ends with another although followed by *śrī śrī*.

A few inscriptions from Karnataka and Orissa also bear representations of floral symbol. The Patna Museum plates of Raṇabhañja (*EI*, XX, p. 10) have at the end a design of a stylized flower with ten petals (fig. 11, *12*).

← Fig. 11. Floral designs: 1 Basim plates of Vākāṭaka Vindhyaśakti II, AD 400; 2 grants of Pravarasena II of Vākāṭaka family; 3 Andhavaram plates of Anantaśakti-varman, fifth century; 4 Kabul inscription of Shāhī Khiṅgala, sixth-seventh century; 5 Talegaon copper plates of Krishṇa-Rāja I, AD 768; 6 Rāshṭrakūṭa record from Cambay, of Govinda IV, AD 930; 7 Chidivalasa plates of Devendravarman, AD 893-895; 8 Masulipatam plates of Chālukya-Bhīma II, AD 934-945; 9 Chebrolu inscription of Jaya; 10 Pillalamarri inscription of the reign of Kāpaya Nāyaka, Śaka 1279; 11 Patnapada grant of Choḍa Bhaktirāja, Śaka 1265; 12 Patna Museum plates of Raṇabhañja; 13 Kendupatna plates of Narasiṁha II, AD 1294; 14 Madras Museum plates of the time of Narendradhavala, tenth century; 15 Ramesvaram inscription of Niśśaṅkamalla, AD 1187; 16 Bodh-Gaya inscription of the time of Sena kings of Bengal

In many respects it is similar to the one noticed in the two inscriptions of Pravarasena II. The Kendupatna plates of Narasiṁha II (AD 1294) (*EI*, XXVIII, p. 185) contain two examples, one with four and the other with eight petals (fig. 11, *13*). A six-petalled flower without the circular thalamus so common in other examples is found in the Madras Museum plates of the time of Narendradhavala (fig. 11, *14*) (*EI*, XXVIII, p. 44) datable to the tenth century. In Karnataka region the floral variety is not so common as the ornamental ones. A four-petalled symbol occurs in one of the Western Chālukyan inscriptions from Dharwar ascribable to the twelfth century (*EI*, XVI, p. 31). Almost similar motif is repeated in an inscription from Mutgi, of the Kālachurya Bhillama, AD 1189 (*EI*, XV, p. 32). The finest representation of a flower, a lotus (fig. 11, *15*), comes from the Ramesvaram inscription of Niśśaṅkamalla (*EI*, XXXVI, p. 23), AD 1187. It is engraved in the centre of the inscription.

It seems that the floral design as an auspicious mark became popular in the area comprising central India, Andhra Pradesh, Orissa, Maharashtra, Gujarat and Karnataka. There is only one example of its occurrence outside this zone: it is from a Bodh-Gaya inscription of the time of the Sena kings of Bengal (*EI*, XII, p. 27). It is an example of a ten-petalled variety drawn at the end of the inscription between the figures of interpunctuation (fig. 11, *16*).

2. Ornamental design

Let it be mentioned at the outset that the ornamental designs are meant to be used only as a decorative symbol and do not possess any individual entity of their own, at least during the medieval times. Again, Andhra Pradesh appears to be the area of concentration, but the time of emergence of this form must be dated posterior to that belonging to the other group. Geographically, however, it covers relatively a wider area, for it is reported as far east as Assam, and on the north Lakha Mandal in the Jaunsar Bawar, Uttar Pradesh.

The ornamental designs display a variety of forms, some of them being of widespread occurrence. Designs having four semicircles and four or eight lines surrounding a pellet are found in Assam, Karnataka, west coast and Rajasthan. This form has been used during the ninth century in the inscriptions from Assam. The Howrahghat plates of Balavarman III of Kāmarūpa, year 5, AD 829 (*EI*, XXXII, p. 283) conclude with this ornamental symbol (fig, 12, *1*), which is noticed also in the Parbatiya plates (fig. 12, *2*) of Vanamālavarmadeva (*EI*, XXIX, p. 145) belonging to the same period. In Karnataka and Rajasthan, the symbol might have been used during the tenth century. It is placed at the commencement of the Hulgur inscription of Khoṭṭiga, a Rāshṭrakūṭa ruler (fig. 12, *3*); the record is dated to AD 972 (*EI*, XXXIV, p. 59). That the motif lingered on in Karnataka till about the twelfth century is apparent from the Asoge plates of Kadamba Jayakeśin (II), AD 1134 (fig. 12, *4*) (*EI*, XXVI, p. 304). In Rajasthan, it is used in the Balera plates of Mūlarāja I (fig. 12, *5*) of the Anhilvad branch of the Chālukyas, AD 995 (*EI*, 8, p. 76). Found also in the Goa region, it is engraved not only at the end, but also in line 6 and 46 (fig. 12, *6*) of the inscription of Kadamba Tribhuvanamalla, AD 1107 (*EI*, XXX, p. 71). An interesting variant of this ornamental design is to be seen in the twelfth-century records (fig. 12, *7*) from district Raipur, Madhya Pradesh (*CII*, IV, part ii, pp. 622-31).

Notwithstanding its wide popularity, the form is absent in the records of the Andhra Pradesh, a region where floral or ornamental symbols had their maximum proliferation. In Andhra Pradesh, however, symbols formed by the combination of pellets and dashes became very popular. The earliest form comprising four pellets surrounding a central one is to be seen in the Pallava record of Kumāravishṇu II (fig. 12, *8*) (*EI*, VIII, p. 233). This very form occurs in the Hottur (Dharwar) inscription (fig. 12, *9*) of the reign of Someśvara I, AD 1067 (*EI*, XVI, p. 81). In the former, the mark appears at the end of line 32, while the latter record opens with it. Subsequently, eight dashes—four emanating, as it were, from the pellets themselves and four more, interspaced—have been added to the basic form. In certain cases, dashes are replaced by wavy lines. Designs of this series are met with in the Vandram (fig. 12, *10*) (*EI*, IX, p. 131), Maliyapundi (fig. 12, *10*) *EI*, IX, p. 47) and Nammuru grants (*EI*, XII, p. 61) of Ammarāja II and in the Ranastipundi grant (fig. 12, *11*) of Vimalāditya (*EI*, VI, p. 347). In the last-mentioned example, the symbol is incised both at the beginning as well as at the end. A slightly modified variant of this form is found in the Atakur inscription of the Western Gaṅga kings Krishṇa III and Būtuga II, AD 949-50 (*EI*, VI, p. 50). Three symbols, all of them being identical, of the Teki plates of Rājarāja Choḍagaṅga, AD 1084 (*EI*, VI, p. 334) may also be taken as a variant of pellet-and-dash motif (fig. 12, *12*).

Three more types of ornamental designs are to be found in the Andhra Pradesh, although they are represented by isolated specimens only. The one occurring at the beginning of the Masulipatam plates of Amma II (AD 945-970) of the Eastern Chālukyan family (*EI*, V, p. 139) has eight wavy lines, as if coming out from a circle (fig. 12, *13*). Like other examples, the floral design is here followed by the word *svasti*. The Akkalapundi grant (fig. 12, *14*) of Siṅgaya Nāyaka, Śaka-*Saṁvat* 1290 (*EI*, XIII, p. 259) and the Vanapalli plates of Anna-Vema, Śaka-*Saṁvat* 1300 (*EI*, III, p. 59) contain quite unfamiliar forms; the inscription "ends with three symbols viz., a lotus

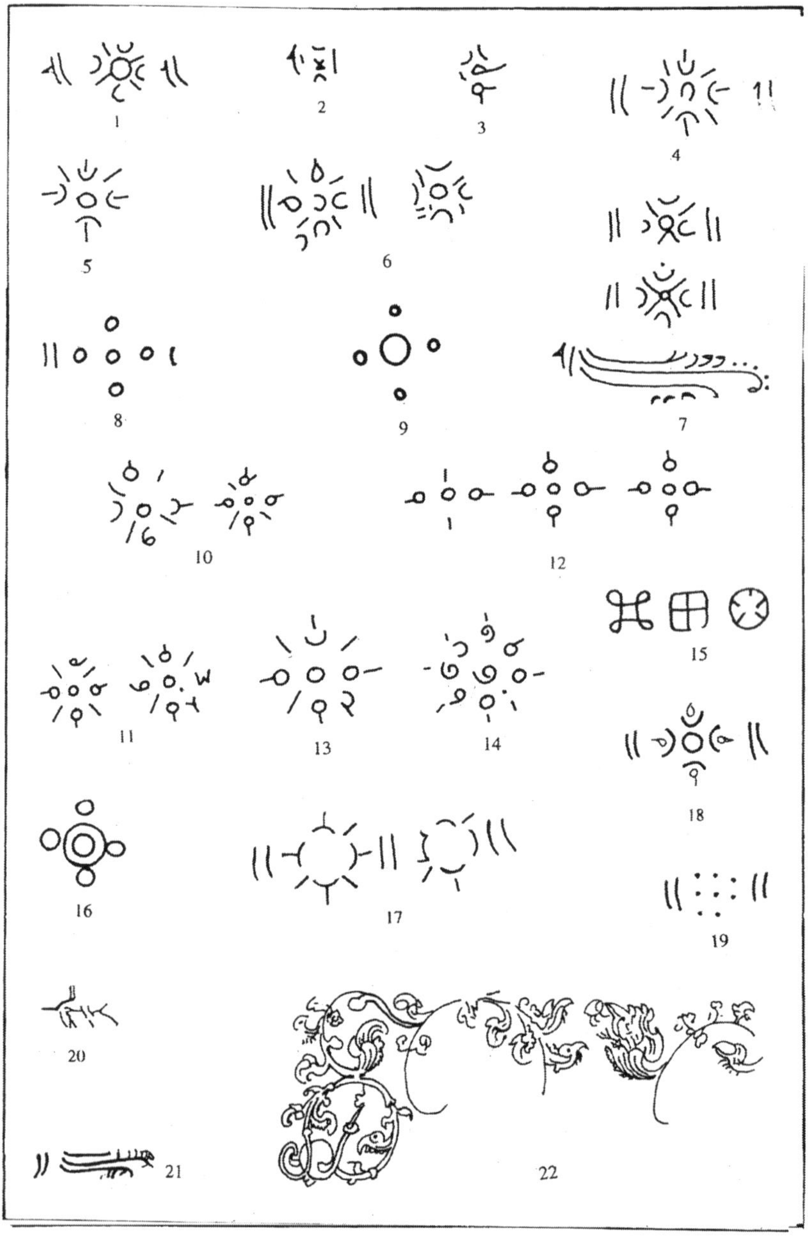

Fig. 12.

flower, a square resembling a *svastika*, and a discus" (fig. 12, *15*). A concentric circle with four pellets at the four directions is a rare symbol occurring in the Donepundi grant of Nāmaya-Nāyaka (fig. 12, *16*), Śaka-*Saṁvat* 1259 (*EI*, V, p. 265 and *EI*, IV, p. 365). Mention may be made about the occurrence of a few more isolated forms noticed variously in the tenth century Sravana-Belgola epitaph of Mārasiṁha II (*EI*, V, p. 151), the Gadivore grant (fig. 12, *17*) of Shashthadeva II, AD 1262 (*EI*, XXXIV, p. 105) and the Dhar *praśasti* of Arjunavarman (fig. 12, *18*) (*EI*, VIII, p. 96). In the last-mentioned examples, one may see the blending of the organic form with the geometrical traditions. The *praśasti* of the temple of Lakhamandal at Madha in Jaunsar Bawar (*EI*, I, p. 10) ends with a symbol consisting of eight pellets encircling a central one (fig. 12, *19*).

It is evident from the foregoing description that symbols with four or eight rays or pellets have generally been used in the inscriptions. The concentration of the ornamental forms in Andhra Pradesh, like the floral ones, may tend to show that they were used also to represent flowers embodying good luck and prosperity. In many instances, the symbol is found in association with the expression *śrī* or prosperity.

3. Vegetal designs

Besides the well-known symbol of tree-within railing mentioned in an earlier chapter a few more vegetal designs are met with in the inscriptions. One such example, a creeper, is found in the Chhoti Sadri stone inscription (fig. 12, *20*) from Rajasthan (*EI*, XXX, p. 120). The inscription, ascribable to the fifth century AD, ends with the representation of a meandering creeper drawn quite realistically. In another instance, a bunch of corn-inflorences

---

← Fig. 12. Floral, ornamental or vegetal symbols: 1 Howraghat plates of Balavarman III of Kāmarūpa, AD 829; 2 Parbatiya plates of Vanamālavarmadeva; 3 Hulgur inscription of Khoṭṭiga, a Rashtrakūṭa ruler AD 972; 4 Asoge plates of Kadamba Jayakeśin (II), AD 1134; 5 Balera plates of Mūlarāja I of the Anahilvad branch of the Chālukyas, AD 995; 6 inscription of Kadamba Tribhuvanamalla, AD 1107; 7 records from Raipur, twelfth century; 8 Pallava record of Kumāravishṇu II; 9 Hottur (Dharwar) inscription of the reign of Someśvara I, AD 1067; 10 Vandram and Maliyapundi grants of Ammarāja II; 11 Ranastipundi grant of Vimalāditya; 12 Teki plates of Rājarāja Choḍagaṅga, AD 1084; 13 Masulipatam plates of Amma II, Eastern Chālukya, AD 945-70; 14 Akkalapundi grants of Siṅgaya Nāyaka, Śaka-Saṁvat 1300; 15 Vanapalli palates of Anna-Vema, Śaka-Saṁvat 1300; 16 Donepundi grants of Nāmaya-Nāyaka, Śaka-Saṁvat 1259; 17 Gadivore grant of Shashṭhadeva II, AD 1262; 18 Dhar *praśasti* of Arjunavarman, thirteenth century AD; 19 *praśasti* of the temple of Lakhamandal at Madha in Jaunsar Bawar, about seventh-eighth century AD; 20 Chhoti Sadri stone inscription; 21 Prince of Museum plates of Dadda III, a Gurjara chief; 22 inscription from Chitaldurg district (*mañjarī*) can also be seen inscribed at the end. It occurs in the Prince of Wales Museum plates (fig. 12, *21*) of Dadda III (*EI*, XXVII, p. 197) a Gurjara chief; the document was issued from Broach in Gujarat and contains the signature of the king followed by the representation of flowering corns.

Trees are considered sacred from prehistoric times and are very often associated with some gods and goddesses. Even this animistic tradition considerably influenced the Buddhist ideology, for every past Buddha, as the Bharhut reliefs show, has his characteristic tree as well. Trees are abodes of *yakshas* or demigods. Each tree has its own spirit too, and every part of it is regarded sacred and auspicious. Symbols which occur in the inscriptions are not, therefore, simple imitation of natural objects. They have their definite purpose and might have been connected with some Indian conception of prosperity and good luck.

In some cases, however, ornamental motif or the floral or vegetal design dominated over the auspicious character. For instance, the ornamental style of writing that developed in the Karnataka region during medieval times made use of different types of meandering motif. The sweeping flourish of some individual letters aimed at providing pictorial effects, and as a mater of fact, in an inscription from Chitaldurg district are recorded (fig. 12, *22*) (*Epi. Car.* XI, No. 47) the claims of the engraver's skill in feats of this kind. In such an artificial arrangement of the letters sometimes the lotus or some flower has been shown within the curls or the loops of the letters. In some cases, the flourish ends in creeper design and weave, a pattern similar to scrolls. The most characteristic example of floral design and scroll-pattern comes from the Sravana-Belgola epitaph of Mallisheṇa, AD 1129 (*EI*, III, p. 194). These are highly stylized motifs and are drawn on the top of the epitaph. Whatever may be their symbolic meaning their main purpose seems to be decorative in nature.

4. General observations

As stated above, the floral design has a very long past notwithstanding its late appearance in Indian epigraphs. Some of the forms noticed in the inscriptions have their distant counterparts in symbols on the ancient coins. According to Allan, there is only one variety of punch-marked silver coins where one finds a definite evidence of the floral design. On tribal coins, however the motif is markedly manifest. Yet one of the ornamental designs of the inscriptions, at least its primary form, is to be seen on silver punch-marked coins. It has been described by Allan as "a pellet surrounded by four semicircles". As one of the most popular device on the punch-marked, cast and tribal coins it is noticed both on the obverse as well as the reverse.

The form occurring in the inscriptions from different areas differs from the coin-device in having dashes around the semicircles. Despite these dissimilarities, a common link between the two series can hardly escape notice.

In later times, as the testimony of inscriptions shows, the symbol with four semicircles around a pellet, was meant to be a flower. Of course, it is not easy to decide whether its earlier prototype carried the same value and the meaning. Alternatively, it may also be a case of old form utilized for a new purpose, with new significance imparted to it. But the former hypothesis seems to be more likely, for in certain types of punch-marked silver coins the symbol is drawn along with an insect which appears to be *bhramara* or wasp. Evidently the symbol depicts the scene of a *bhramara* attracted by the smell and colour of a flower. In the circumstances, one has to identify this symbol—occurring frequently on the ancient Indian coins—as a flower.

The form of the symbol does not reveal any naturalistic representation; it is a clear example of geometrical abstraction. But the study of the floral designs has already shown that even the geometrical forms do stand for a floral motif. The majority of the highly abstract figures of the inscriptions share one common feature: a circle or a circle with a dot in the centre. As indicated, the circle possibly represents the thalamus on which other floral members stand and survive. It serves as a platform for the pollen-bearing stamen and the female-organ bearing carpel to unite. So, a circle with a dot or concentric circles represent union, procreation, proliferation and prosperity. This explains also the association of the floral symbol with *śrī* or prosperity in several epigraphs: expressions like *maṅgala mahāśrī*, *śrī śrī śrī* and *svasti śrīḥ* are quite significant in this context.

It is also interesting to note that where the floral or ornamental symbol occurs at the opening, in many instances, it is preceded or followed by the word *svasti*, and not *siddhaṁ* or *Oṁ*. Perhaps it implies complimentary present of flower as a token of good luck.

It appears from what has been said above that the apparent meaning of the symbols, together with their geometrical forms, may be taken as a flower. A deeper significance however lies hidden beneath its simple appearance: it is a sign of prosperity, it symbolizes union of two vital forces. In religious practices, circle is conceived as a cosmos; circles with four or eight rays are objects of meditation. Many of the floral designs in the inscriptions possibly betray this aspect of symbolism, for they have in several cases four or eight petals.

The most popular types of the Andhra Pradesh region as well as of the Lakha Mandal are made in combination of pellets or dots—such symbols being noticed also on the ancient Indian coins. These are, nevertheless, quite elementary forms, and like any other geometrical pattern, might have reappeared in response to some similar conditions. But one, with four semicircles and dashes surrounding an orb or pellet, does not appear to be of elementary type; its long chain of evolution may, therefore, be regarded as the continuity of the same tradition in spite of the fact that its inner meaning might have undergone some change. Outwardly and in apparent meaning it remained an abstract flower, an auspicious mark, a sign of prosperity and good luck. Even the vegetal motifs like green foliage, meandering creepers and flowering cores, which have their use even today in religious rites and ceremonies, are taken as auspicious signs and are regarded as harbingers of success and fortune.

Notes and References

1. J.N. Banerjea, *The Development of Hindu Iconography* (Calcutta, 1956), pp. 403, 557.
2. D.C. Sircar, 'Chidivalasa plates of Devendravarman; Gaṅga year 397', *Journal of the Asiatic Society of Bengal* (Letters), Vol. XVIII (1952), pp. 77-81, pl. III.
3. P. Sreenivasachar, *A Corpus of Inscriptions in the Telingana District of H.E.H. The Nizam's Dominions*, Hyderabad Archaeological Series, No. 13

CHAPTER 6

WHEEL AND CONCH-SHELL

As evident from the foregoing pages, it is not always easy to visualize the inner meaning and significance of the early symbols. Sometimes it is not even possible to understand their immediate or obvious meaning because of too much distortion of forms and rejection of essential details in the examples of the later period. Yet many of them might have been copied from familiar objects of nature but their presentation in cryptic form makes it difficult to establish their relationship with the originals. These symbols being far removed from their originals have no naturalistic appearance, nor do their outward forms provide any pictorial appeal. But this trend showed signs of gradual transformation during the early Christian era when symbols, with more or less natural forms made their emergence felt even in the epigraphical records. Side by side, the earlier symbols like *triratna, svastika,* etc., had also their use. By that time, however, they had acquired specific connotations though under specific conditions. Some of them entered into the domain of philosophical speculation as symbolic terms expressing various concepts and cosmological phenomena.

Wheel, flower and conch-shell appeared in the inscriptions of India in this period of naturalistic representation of symbols. Here the obvious meaning is quite understandable in spite of the fact that their hidden significance may not always be clear unless the context in which they are used is known. The change took place in a period when visual art of the country reached great heights and this might have cast influence in moulding the external forms of the symbols.

1. Wheel or *chakra*

The realistic representation of wheel is an old motif and it occurs occasionally on the ancient coins, and also on pottery. Two varietes of wheels are found in obverse types of silver punch-marked coins; one of the types has been identified as a water-wheel. The other type is a simple eight-spoked one

Fig. 13. Wheel or *chakra*: 1 Mathura stone image inscription of Kumāragupta I, AD 454-55; 2 Nachne-ki-Talai inscription of Mahārāja Prithvishena, Vākāṭaka ruler; 3 Vākāṭaka inscription from Ganj; 4 Jodhpur inscription of Pratihāra Bāuka, Vikrama-Saṁvat 894 (AD 837); 5 Torkhede copper-plate grant of the time of Govindarāja, Śaka-Saṁvat 735 (AD 812); 6 Pilgrim's record in a Kākatiya inscription from Gayā, twelfth-thirteenth century; 7 Krishnapuram plate of the Vijayanagara king Sadāśivarāya, Śaka-Saṁvat 1489; 8 inscription of Jishṇugupta, from Nepal.

with a circular hub. A wheel on the reverse of Achyuta coins, datable to the fourth century AD, has eight spokes emanating from an inner ring with a solid circular hub.[1] But the earliest representation of *chakra* in an epigraph is the Mathura stone-image inscription (fig. 13, *1*) (*CII*, III, p. 262), AD 454-55, of Kumāragupta I. It is engraved on the margin at the commencement of the record and represents a fifteen-spoked double-rimmed wheel with a circular hub in the centre. An eight-spoked wheel is found also in the centre of a four-lined inscription of Vyāghradeva from Nachne-ki-Talai (fig. 13, *2*; pl. V) belonging to the time of Mahārāja Prithivishena, the Vākāṭaka ruler (*CII*, V, p. 89). Another Vākāṭaka inscription, of Vyāgharadeva, from Ganj (fig. 13, *3*; pl. VI) (*CII*, V, p. 92) has, in the centre of the first line, a wheel in which only three spokes are visible. Perhaps it was intended to be an eight-spoked one like the other Vākāṭaka examples. Both the examples, however, are in relief. But certainly they have been used as a symbol possibly denoting Vaishṇava affiliation.

The wheel is noticed also in a few medieval records. An eight-spoked wheel and a conch-shell are represented at the end of line 21 of the Jodhpur inscription of Pratihāra Bauka, AD 837 (fig. 13, *4*) (*EI*, XVIII, p. 87). In certain cases it is represented by a four-spoked variety, which is also the mark for the numeral 90. It is also found on the Harappan seals and as graffiti on chalcolithic and megalithic pottery.[2] But similarity of forms does not necessarily imply that all of them expressed the same symbolic meaning. For instance, this symbol in medieval inscriptions meant the discus, an emblem of Vishṇu; perhaps it has been used in the same context in the Torkhede copper-plate grant of the time of Govindarāja[3] (fig. 13, *5*), Śaka Saṁvat 735 (*EI*, III, p. 53) and as one of the three symbols in the Vanapalli plates of Anna-Vema, a Reḍḍi king of Koṇḍavīḍu, AD 1380 (*EI*, III, p. 59). Without any doubt, the wheel alongwith a *śaṅkha* on a pedestal in a Kākatīya inscription (fig. 13, *6*; pl. VIII), a pilgrim's record from Gaya is meant to be the sacred Vaishṇava symbol. The inscription of the time of Pratāparudra I is dated to the twelfth-thirteenth centuries (*EI*, XXXIII, p. 103). Again, on the top of the Krishnapuram plates of the Vijayanagara king Sadāśivarāya, Śaka Saṁvat 1489 (*EI*, IX, p. 328) and immediately above the inscription is engraved the *Śrīvaishnava nāmaṁ* (of the Tangalai sect) (fig. 13, *7*) flanked on either side by the conch and discus or *chakra*, evidently representing the emblems of Vishṇu.

But wheel is not necessarily a Vaishṇava insignia. At the beginning it might have been used as a solar symbol in different parts of the globe. In some Nepalese inscriptions, it has been used as an auspicious symbol denoting sun-wheel. For instance, an undated inscription of Jishṇugupta from Nepal, has on its top a *chakra* with flames around.[4] As is well-known, the Buddhists were primarily responsible for popularising it as *dharma-chakra*. For the Vaishṇavas, it is a fatal weapon, *Sudarśana*, and for its popularity the Gupta monarchs of the fourth-fifth centuries contributed greatly. The practice of engraving the sculpture of wheel above the inscription is noticed also in the Susunia rock-inscription of Chandravarman, datable to the fifth-sixth centuries.[5] In course of time, the *chakra* was glorified to such an extent as to assume an anthropomorphic form as one of the *āyudhapurushas*. Yet it has to be admitted that despite its religious importance its occurrence in inscriptions, and also on coins, is only few and far between.

2. *Śaṅkha* or conch-shell

The *śaṅkha* or conch-shell is another sacred attribute of Vishṇu but it has hardly been used in inscriptions prior to medieval times. There are actual specimens of *śaṅkha* inscribed with the name of one of the forms of Vishṇu, datable to the third century, yet as an auspicious mark it has rarely been used on ancient coins or as pottery motif. Of course, spirals representing the shell-whorl seem to be one of the earliest symbols that mankind made use of. Like the *chakra* it too was idealized as one of the *āyudhapurushas*, and in some period of development of this symbol it became associated with Kubera, the god of wealth, as one of his *nidhis*.

Symbols represented in inscriptions do not, however, present any evolutionary picture that has been drawn above. What one finds there is either a naturalistic or a stylized representation of *śaṅkha*, the earliest examples of which are datable to the seventh century. In the majority of cases, the symbol occupies the left margin of the record. One of the two Kalachuri grants containing the inscription of Tejavarman datable to AD 709-10 issued during the rule of Pṛithivīchandra Bhogaśakti (fig. 14, *1*; pl. VII A) from Anjaneri (*EI*, XXV, p. 225) has a fine representation of *śaṅkha*. The symbol is noticed in the margin of the plates of Dantivarman below an intertwined design (fig. *11*) (*EI*, VI, p. 285), Lucknow Museum plate of Kīrtipāla, AD 1111 (fig. 14, *7*; pl. XIV) (*EI*, VII, p. 93) and in the Kottayam plate of Vīra-Rāghava (fig. 14, *6*) (*EI*, IV, p. 290). In some inscriptions, the symbol has been drawn either at the beginning or at the end. One of the twelfth century epigraphs at Narendra, district Dharwar (*EI*, XIII, p. 298) opens with the representation of *śaṅkha* followed by *Śrī Oṁ Namaś-Śivāya* and has at the end a spiral symbol, a *daṇḍa*, and a *śaṅkha*. The Jodhpur inscription of Pratihāra Bauka, AD 837 (fig. 14, *4*) (*EI*, XVIII, p. 87) contains representation of a *śaṅkha* at the end of line 21 (fig. 14, *5*). A Pabhosa inscription (*EI*, II, p. 480) also has this symbol in between lines 3 and 4 (fig. 14, *2*) though preceded by another *maṅgala* (pl. VII B). But it is engraved in the last line of the Bihapur inscription of Dhavala of Hastikundi (*EI*, X, p.17). A Western Chālukyan record from Kurgod, Bellary (*EI*, XIV, p. 265) has, in its 44th line, no less than three *śaṅkhas* (fig. 14, *4*); another inscription incised just below the previous one, however, starts with it.

It appears that conch-shell became popular as a symbol in the inscriptions between about the eighth century and the fourteenth century. The Kākatīya inscription from Gaya (*EI*, XXXIII, p. 103) and the Vijayanagara inscription mentioned above have representations of *śaṅkha* on top. Two late medieval records from Orissa—copper plate grant from Balasore (fig. 14, *8*) (*IA*, I, p. 355) and Bandh grant of Raṇabhañjadeva (fig. 14, *9*) (*EI*, XII, p. 322) show the side view of the conch-shell, similar

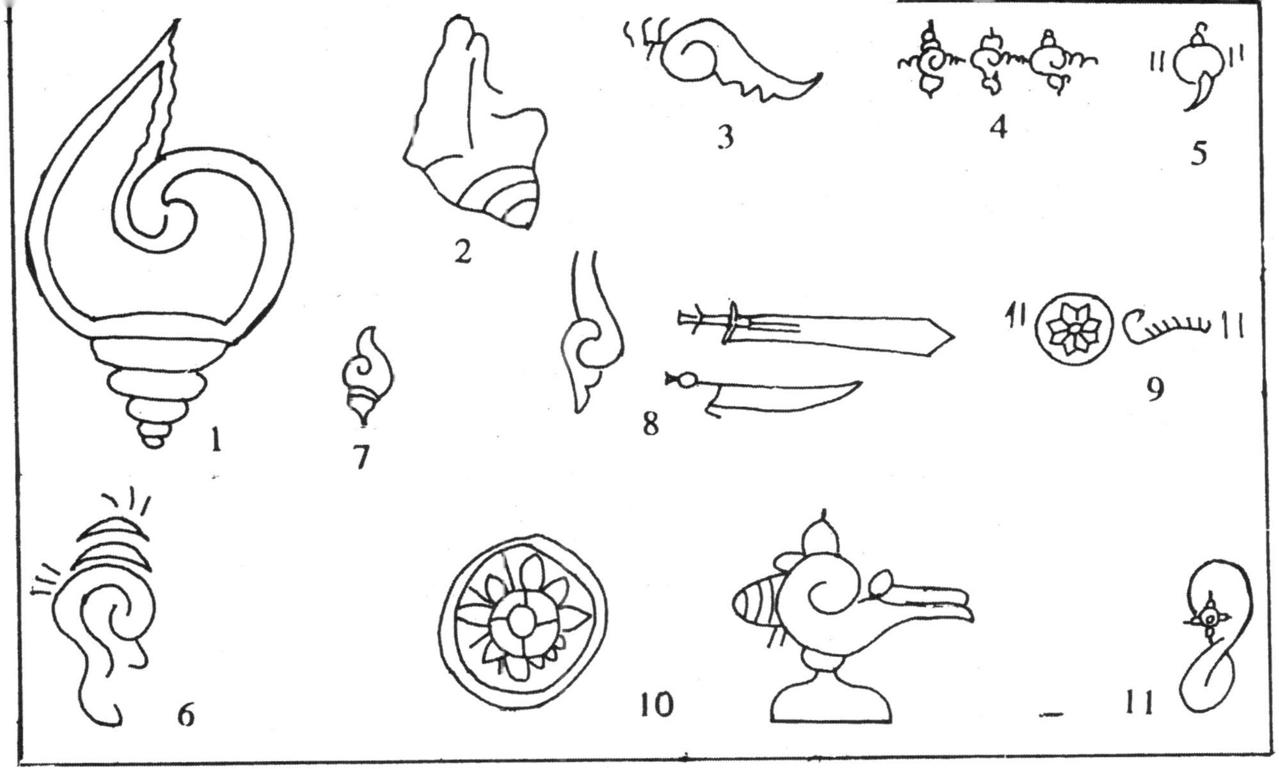

Fig. 14. *Śaṅkha* or conch-shell: 1 grant of Prithivīchandra Bhogaśakti, Kalachuri ruler, from Anjaneri, AD 709-10; 2 Pabhīsa inscription, circa seventh-eighth century AD; 3 Chidivalasa plates of Devendravarman, Gaṅga year 397, ninth century; 4 Western Chālukya record from Kurgod, Bellary, twelfth century; 5 Jodhpur inscription of Pratihāra Bāuka, AD 837; 6 Kottayam plate of Vīra Rāghava, circa fourteenth century AD; 7 Lucknow Museum plate of Kīrtipāla, AD 1111; 8 copper plate grant from Balasore, Orissa; 9 Baudh grant of Raṇabhañjadeva, 54th year of Bhañja dynasty; 10 inscription of the time of Kākatīya Pratāparudra I, thirteenth century, from Gaya; 11 Kolur inscription of the reign of Yādava Siṅghana, thirteenth century

representation being found in ninth century record—Chidivalasa plates of Devendravarman, Gaṅga year 395[5] (fig. 14, *3*).

Mention may be made of an interesting variety of the *śaṅkha*-symbol noticed in the Kolur inscription of the reign of Singhana (*EI*, XIX, p. 194) datable to the twelfth century AD (fig. 14, *11*). Here it is represented wholly by a stylized form, with an ornamental symbol as its mouth. The symbol stands at the opening of line 24, and was obviously meant to be an auspicious mark. An inscription of the time of Kākatīya Pratāparudra I, from Gaya (*EI*, XXXIII, 103) has, at the end of the inscription, representations of the *chakra* (discus) and *śaṅkha* (conch-shell), the latter on pedestal (fig. 14, *10*; pl. VIII).

It is doubtful if the *śaṅkha* symbol stood for an emblem of Vishnu though of course it is found flanking the *Śrīvaishṇava nāmaṁ* on the top of the Krishnapuram plates of the Vijayanagara king Sadāśivarāya (see above, fig. 13, 7). As it occurs in the medieval records, the possibility of its association with the *śaṅkha-nidhi* of Kubera cannot be wholly discounted. It is found at the beginning of a Śaiva epigraph as well. All this may indicate that this symbol, like lotus, spiral and *svastika* was used also as a *maṅgala*. The tradition is followed also in some inscriptions from Nepal.

But the symbol has not been used in India extensively as it appears to have been confined to parts of south Karnataka, Orissa, eastern Uttar Pradesh and Rajasthan.

Inscriptional data do not, however, bring out fully the magical and religious associations that conch-shells and shell-objects have had in India from a very remote past. It is a living symbol in Brahmanical rites and ceremonies and is often used in different parts of India to ward off evil effects. Very often different components like artificial lips, columulla, etc., are used for magical purposes. On the other hand, this aspect has never been touched upon, as inscriptions generally show the full representation of the *śaṅkha*. All this may suggest that the magical or ritualistic ideas connected with the conch-shell did not find any expression in the representation of *śaṅkha* in different Indian epigraphs.

Notes and References

1. J. Allan, *A Catalogue of the Indian Coins in the British Museum,* p. 117.
2. B.B. Lal, 'From the Megalithic to the Harappa: tracing back the graffiti on the pottery', *Ancient India*, No. 16 (1960) pl. XXI.
3. However, this symbol could have represented *Oṁ* in this inscription as suggested by the editor of the inscription.
4. Bhagvanlal Indraji, *Twenty-three Inscriptions from Nepal* (Bombay, 1885), p. 11, Ins. No. 10, plate facing p. 11.
5. D.C. Sircar, *Indian Epigraphy* (1965), p. 96.
6. D.C Sircar, 'Chidivalasa plates of Devendravarman, Gaṅga year 397', *Journal of the Asiatic Society of Bengal* (Letters), XVIII, p. 77, pl. I.

CHAPTER 7

MISCELLANEOUS SYMBOLS

Several marks and representations in inscriptions which do not fall under any broad category have been included in this chapter. Undoubtedly, many of them are symbols though their individual meaning and significance is not easily intelligible. These symbols include circle, star, intertwined design, criss-cross pattern, marks resembling Brāhmī letters and conventional representations as signatures.

1. The circle

Circles and concentric circles have been noticed in a number of inscriptions, the earliest of which dates back to the fifth century AD. The symbol occurs both at the beginning as well as at the end, the latter being the common practice. Apart from simple circles, examples of double and concentric circles have also come to light. The Chhoti Sadri stone-inscription from Rajasthan (*EI*, XXX, p. 120) ascribable to the fifth century AD has, in line 17, two concentric circles (fig. 15, *1*), while a record from Kausambi, Pali copper-plate grant of Mahārāja Lakshmaṇa (*EI*, II, p. 363) of 5th-6th century AD opens with the symbol of circle (fig. 15, *2*). There is another inscription where the record starts with a circle; it is in the Srirangam plates of Vīra-Harihara-Rāya-Uḍaiyar (III), Śaka 1336 (fig. 15, *3*) (*EI*, XVI, p. 222). In several other cases, the symbol is drawn at the end. The Bandh plates of Salonabhañja datable to the fourteenth century (*EI*, XXVI, p. 276) end with a circle placed in between two sets of *daṇḍas* (fig. 15, *4*). This placement in between the marks of punctuation reveals its symbolic character. A circle occurs at the end of line 61 of the Kharepatan plates of Raṭṭarāja, AD 1008-9 (*EI*, III, p. 292); here, too, the symbol is placed in between the two sets of *daṇḍas* (fig. 15, *5*). In the Bichapalli Western Chālukyan inscription of Bhuvanaikamalla's time, AD 1074 (*EI*, XXXVI, p. 69) two double circles mark the end of the epigraph (fig. 15, *6*).

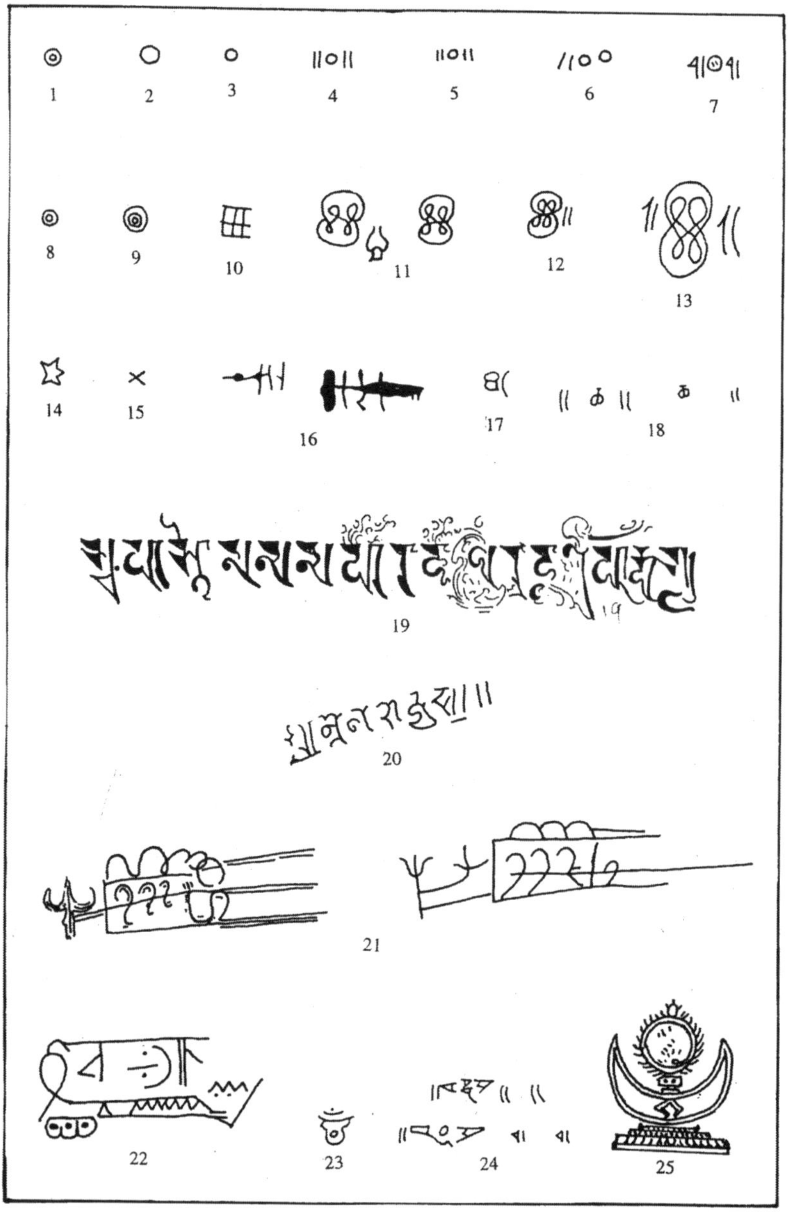

Fig. 15

Sometimes concentric circles have been used at the end of the inscription: one of the three grants from Chinchani (*EI*, XXXII, p. 61) has a concentric circle in between the two sets of double *daṇḍas*: (fig. 15, *7*), the first punctuation mark of each set looks like the English numeral four. The Begur inscription of Ereyappa, AD 908 and 938 (*EI*, VI, p. 45), also contains double concentric circles (fig. 15, *8*). An example of triple concentric circles comes from the Jaina rock-inscriptions at Vallimalai, Śaka-Saṁvat 899 (fig. 15, *9*) (*EI*, IV, p. 140); the two last-mentioned records belong to the Western Gaṅga dynasty of Karnataka.

It is evident from the above that circles and concentric circles have been used in the inscriptions from the fifth to the fourteenth centuries more as symbols than as marks of punctuation or simple ornamentation. But the symbol has been used to mark the end of a section or as a full-stop, like any other symbol such as *svastika*, flower, etc.[1] Evidently, the mark has been utilized out of the common repository of ancient Indian symbolism. It occurs as graffiti on the chalcolithic and megalithic pottery,[2] as an important component of various well-known devices on ancient coins, in religious images, instruments of meditation, *yantra* of the Tantric practices, as the central part of several floral and ornamental designs, etc. In higher philosophical and cosmological speculations it represents the universe, the cosmos. Its use at the opening of the records and at the conclusion may indicate its auspicious or magical character; it is invoked with a view to bring the desired result.

← Fig. 15. 1 Chhoti Sadri stone inscription, fifth century AD; 2 Pali copper plate grant of Mahārāja Lakshmaṇa (Saṁvat 158) fifth-sixth century; 3 Srirangam plates of Vīra-Harihara-Rāya-Udaiyar (III), Śaka 1336; 4 Bandh plates of Salonabhañja, fourteenth century; 5 Kharepatan plates of Raṭṭarāja, AD 1008-9; 6 Bichapalli western Chālukyan inscription of Bhuvanaikamalla's time, AD 1074; 7 Rashṭrakuṭa grant from Chinchani, Śaka 848 (AD 926); 8 Begur inscription of Eṛeyappa, AD 908 and 938; 9 Jain rock-inscriptions at Vallimalai, Śaka-Saṁvat 899; 10 Khanapur plates of Mādhavavarman, seventh century AD; 11 plates of Dantivarman of Gujarat, Śaka Saṁvat 789; 12 Prince of Wales Museum plates of Govindarāja, AD 810; 13 copper-plate of Dhruva II of the Gujarat Rāshṭrakūṭa branch, AD 884; 14 Akkalkot inscription of Śilāhāra Indarasa, western Chālukya, AD 1114; 15 Jodhpur plates of the time of Durlabhharāja, Vikrama-Saṁvat 1069 (AD 1013); 16 Velur rock-inscription of Nolamba king Kannaradeva, AD 940-956; 17 Orissa plates of Vidyādharabhañja-deva, circa twelfth-thirteenth century; 18 Kamauli plate of Govindachandra [Vikrama] Saṁvat 1182 (AD 1126); 19 Banskhera plate of Harsha, early seventh century; 20 Balera plates of Mūlarāja I, AD 995 ; 21 Chiruvroli grant of Hambīra, Śaka 1383; 22 grant of Raghudeva, Śaka 1378; 23 Kanker plates of Pamparājadeva, AD 1213-14; 14 Saheth-Maheth plate of Govinda Chandra AD 1128-29; 25 Mehar plate of Dāmodaradeva, AD 1234

2. Criss-cross design

Only one example of a criss-cross design is known from the inscriptions; it is the Khanapur plates of Mādhavavarman from district Satara, Maharashtra (*EI*, XXVII, p. 312). Datable to the sixth century AD, the epigraph ends with the criss-cross symbol in which three parallel lines are intersected by three vertical ones (fig. 15, *10*). It gives rise to four squares, the horizontal lines extending on either side beyond the verticals. In all likelihood, it is a very ancient symbol, for it is noticed as graffito on Harappan, chalcolithic and megalithic pottery.[3] But the number of squares in the symbol of the latter series is generally more than four. A four-squared symbol may, however, be noticed as an obverse device of 'a very distinctive little group' of punch-marked silver coins.[4] It seems, therefore, that arrangements of squares in the aforesaid inscription might have been drawn from an ancient tradition.

3. Endless knot design

Whether the design represents intertwined snakes or something else is difficult to say. Such intertwined motifs are commonly met with in the popular art of *alpanā* i.e. the art of decorating floor or ground with dried or wet rice-powder still now prevalent in different parts of India. It may be mentioned here that intertwined snakes are also considered auspicious in Indian tradition and sometimes the motif occurs also in plastic art.

This symbol is noticed only in the Rāshṭrakūṭa records from Gujarat, all of them belonging to the ninth century. In the plates of Dantivarman, Śaka-Saṁvat 789 (*EI*, VI, p. 285), the design is engraved in duplicate below the inscription along with a representation of a *śaṅkha* (fig. 15,*11*). It is found in the middle of line 52 of the Prince of Wales Museum plates of Govindarāja, AD 810 (fig. 15, *12*) (*EI*, XXVI, p. 248). Again, the design is engraved between the lines 69 and 70 (last line), after the signature and before the word *lekhitaṁ*, in the copper-plate of Dhruva II of the Gujarat Rāshṭrakūṭa branch (fig. 15, *13*; pl. IX) (*EI*, XXII, p. 64). The inscription is dated to AD 883.

4. The star

The star of this kind is a rare symbol in inscriptions and on coins. It, however, occurs in the Akalkot inscription of Śilāhāra Indarasa, a Western Chāḷukyan record from Dharwar (*EI*, XXVII, p. 65) and is dated to AD 1114. The star shows five radiating points (fig. 15, *14*). Sometimes the symbol occurs in inscriptions from Nepal.

5. The cross and vertical lines

There are cases where the inscription ends with a cross sign or a group of vertical lines. For instance, the Jodhpur plates of the time of Durlabharāja, AD 1013 (*EI*, XXXVI, p. 95) has this at the conclusion of the record. The cross (fig. 15, *15*) here is like a sign of multiplication and perhaps indicates fullstop. Generally, one, two, or four vertical lines at the end may show the end of the record. Sometimes tilde or swung dash is used at the end after a symbol is incised. Mention may be made about the occurrence of vertical lines in the Valur rock-inscription of Nolamba king Kannaradeva, AD 940-956 (*EI*, IV, p. 81). Here the epigraph opens with three vertical lines followed by a horizontal (fig. 15, *16*) mark the end of the record.

The cross is used in later inscriptions as a mark of omission; this cross is known as *kākapāda* or *haṁsapāda*.[5] But in the case of Jodhpur plates of Durlabharāja, Vikrama 1013 (*EI*, XXXVI, p. 95), it was certainly not used as a mark of omission; perhaps its use was like that of a *svastika, triratna* or floral symbol. Thus, the possibility of its use as a symbol cannot be overlooked especially when its antiquity stretches back to chalcolithic and megalithic times as graffiti marks on pottery.[6] Likewise, three or four vertical lines at the beginning or at the end may be taken as a symbol. And these are very old symbols, for they occur on the pottery from the Harappan to the megalithic times. Lal has shown that each of the symbols consisting variously of two, three, four and five parallel vertical lines, form distinct variety.[7]

6. Symbols resembling Brāhmī alphabets

There are some marks appearing generally at the end which closely resemble some Brāhmī letters. Even the taurine symbols in the Jaugada edicts have been taken by several scholars as Brāhmī *ma*. But the symbols similar to Brāhmī alphabets that one comes across in later inscriptions possibly bear some significance. Thus, in the Saheth-Maheth plate of Govindachandra, AD 1128-29 (*EI*, XI, p. 20), one finds a symbol which looks like the letter *gha* found in the same epigraph. Similarly, the Orissa plates of Vidyādharabhañjadeva (*EI*, IX, p. 271) have at the end a mark (fig. 15, *17*) very much resembling the letter *tha* of the period. Again, some of the copper-plates of the kings of Kanauj (*EI*, IV, pp. 97-129: inscriptions C, E and N) end with a sign simulating *chha* of the same records (fig. 15, *18*). They were undoubtedly used as a symbol, but the form, due to some reason or the other, became very similar to the one in prevailing Brāhmī letters. The explanation that D.C. Sircar has provided for this apparent similarity appears to be quite plausible. According to him: "As the circle with a central dot is the old Brāhmī letter *tha*, modified forms of the same letter came to be used in later times. In some medieval records, the symbol stands midway between *tha* and *cha*, and this confusion led to the growth of the popular use of the letter *cha* as the concluding mark at the end of literary or epigraphic records and sections thereof. *Cha* is recognized in this capacity in early medieval works like Śrīharṣa's *Naiṣadhīya* and Hemacandra's *Ekākṣarakoṣa*. Sometimes the auspicious word *śrī* also appears in the same way at the end of documents."[8] In other words, these Brāhmī alphabets, sometimes repeated thrice, represent the circle or circle with a dot.

7. Conventional representation of signature

Several procedures were adopted to ensure the genuineness of a charter; one of the commonest device was to attest it with a royal seal. But no less common was the practice of inscribing a royal signature at the end as a mark of authentication. The practice possibly started some time in the sixth century, as is evident from the Palitana plates of Siṁhāditya, a Maitraka record from Kathiawad datable to AD 574 (*EI*, XI, p. 16). Here the last line runs as: *Svahasto mama* or 'by my own hand'. The grant of Dadda III, AD 675 (*EI*, XXVII, p. 197) has at the end; *sva-hasto mama śrī Daddasya* followed by a vegetal motif. Harsha's Banskhera plate (*EI*, IV, p. 208) bears almost the same formula (fig. 15, *19*). But the Balera plate of Mūlarāja I, AD 995 (*EI*, X, p. 76), of the Anhilvad branch of the Chaulukyas, ends with a flower followed by *Śrī Mūlarājasya* (fig. 15, *20*) while the records of the Chandella king Madanavarmmadeva, AD 1136, have the formula *sva-hasto='yaṁ śrīman Madanavarmmadevasya matam mama*[9] (*EI*, XXXII, p. 123). In the Vijayanagara records, the name of the tutelary deity, expressed variously as *Śrī Virupāksha, Śrī Tryambaka, Śrī Venkaṭeśa, Śrī Harihara, Śrī Rāmachandra,* is met with. But the most interesting form is found in the grants of the Sūryavaṁśī Gajapatis of Orissa in which a stylized representation of a dagger or sword takes the place of the royal signatures. The representation possibly stands for the king's signatures on the original document and later inscribed on the copper plates. The Chiruvroli grant of Hambīra, Śaka 1383 (*EI*, XXXIV, p. 177) has this representation on the reverse of the first plate as well as on the fourth and fifth plates (fig. 15, *21*). Evidently, the sword here stands as a symbol of royal authority. A grant of Raghudeva, who was the governor of Rajahmundry during the reign of Gajapati Kapileśvāra, between AD 1455 and 1460, has, at the end of one of the grants viz., Raghudevapura grant of Śaka 1378, (*EI*, XXXIII, p. 2), three floral designs. Below the inscription in the right hand part of the space is an ornamental design which was "the symbolical representation of the donor's signature on the original document later incised on the plates" (fig. 15, *22*).

8. Bull-head with crescent

Of this symbol, the most definite part is a crescent. The rest appears to be a stylized representation of a bull. Found in the Kanker copper-plates of Pamparājadeva, AD 1213-14, from Chhatisgarh (fig. 15, *23*), the figure is engraved at the end of the record (*EI*, IX, p. 166). The editor of the inscription has identified it as representing the moon, and he thinks it to be the family crest. But the possibility of its being a bull-head with a crescent cannot also be ruled out. In that case, the bull represents the Śiva, and the symbol stands for Śiva's Śaśāṅkaśekhara aspect.

9. Representation of bird's wing

A symbol looking like a bird's wing is found engraved at the end of the Saheth-Maheth (fig. 15, *24*) plate of Govinda Chandra (*EI*, XI, p. 20), the Gāhaḍavāla king. The symbol is followed by two vertical strokes and another symbol in the form of the letter *gha* found in the same inscription dated to AD 1128-29.

10. Miscellaneous

The Mehar plate of Dāmodaradeva, AD 1234 (*EI*, XXVII, p. 182) has on the reverse side on top of the plate, the representation of "a rayed disc of the sun set upon and inside a crescent" (fig. 15, *25*) while it has on the obverse the representation of "Vishṇu on Garuḍa or in the angry attitude of slaying a fallen foe".

It is not easy to exhaust the list of symbols and symbolic representations in the inscriptions. Nor is it possible always to identify even the outward meaning, let alone its inner significance. Further, Indian epigraphy is a dynamic subject, and many more evidence that will come to light in future may also help in deciphering the real significance of several less-known symbols.

Notes and References

1. According to D.C. Sircar: "Often the end of an epigraph was indicated by punctuation marks and occasionally the end of a sentence or section or the first or second half of a stanza was also likewise marked. At the end of a section, sometimes we have the representation of a lotus, a floral design, a

circle and other symbols". See, his *Indian Epigraphy* (1965), pp. 5-6. Elsewhere, in the same work (p. 94) he writes: "In early medieval epigraphs and manuscripts, a circle, with a smaller circle or dot (or dots) inside, sometimes indicate full stop".

2. Lal, 'From the Megalithic to the Harappa: tracing back the graffiti on the pottery', *Ancient India*, No. 16 (1960), pl. XX.
3. Lal, *ibid.,* pl. IX.
4. J. Allan, *A Catalogue of the Indian Coins in the British Museum*, p. XXXIV.
5. D.C. Sircar, *op.cit.* (1965), p. 91 writes, "In later inscriptions and manuscripts, this spot of omission was indicated often by a small upright or inclined cross, generally called *kāka-pāda* or *haṁsa-pāda*. Instead of the cross, the *svastika* symbol was also used".
6. Lal, *op.cit.*, pl. IX.
7. Lal, *ibid.*, pls. XXIV, XXV.
8. D.C. Sircar, *op.cit.* (1965), p. 94.
9. *Ibid.*, p. 148.

CHAPTER 8

GRAPHIC REPRESENTATIONS

In the preceding pages an attempt has been made to classify and discuss the conventionalized forms of symbols appearing in Indian epigraphs. The present chapter is devoted primarily to those types which have more or less naturalistic forms; their use in the majority of the cases was that of a symbol, with an apparent and inner meaning. Here there is not much basic distortion of forms, not much departure from reality. In certain cases, they do reveal artistic quality as well. The sculptural tradition of India is full of such symbolic representations and narrations; indeed, symbolism is practically the core and kernal of Indian plastic art.

1. Animal symbolism

Animal symbolism has a great profusion in religion and art of all times. Even its contribution in the development of various scripts is not negligible; several Egyptian and other hieroglyphs, Chinese characters, Sinaitic and cuneiform scripts, etc., are derived from the animal world. Fishes and snakes, likewise, have also been used in symbolic and pictographic art which may be regarded as the preliminary stage of writing. All these are far removed from the actualities, and are similar to those described in the preceding pages. Yet many of these forms developed from some kind of primitive naturalistic drawings. It need not be emphasized that primitive and prehistoric paintings have often easily recognisable views of animals. Generally animals served as tribesman's totem; their behaviour often inexplicable to the forbears aroused awe and admiration. Their movements were copied in dance, their characteristic features copied in masks, paintings and magical rites. All this clearly shows how deep was the impact of animal symbolism on human behaviour and culture.

In Indian myths, mythology and folklore, animals play significant roles. They personify gods and goddesses; their behaviour was that of a human

Fig. 16. Gajatame, Aśokan rock-edict, Kalsi, third century BC

being. In plastic representations an animal figure is not merely a mute spectator introduced by an artist to impart balance of beauty to the scene but is a real character symbolizing an idea, a god or a goddess. Despite the popularity of animal motifs in Indian art and religions early Indian epigraphs rarely portray an animal figure. As a part of the imprecatory scenes of the late medieval periods, the cow with her calf, the bull and sometimes the donkey or the pig figure in the records of Karnataka, central India and Orissa. But so far as early inscriptions are concerned there are only a few examples in spite of the fact that the practice was introduced by Aśoka as early as the third century BC. The elephant with coiled trunk in the Kalsi rock-edict (*EI*, II, p. 461) is the earliest such graphic representation in an Indian epigraph (fig. 16; pl. XI A). It has been labelled as *gajatame*, the supreme elephant, and symbolically represents Buddha. As the extant label shows, even the Girnar rock-edict might have had a similar colophon though with a different title, *śvetahasti* or 'white elephant.' It is believed that the Great Master in the form of a white elephant entered the womb of his mother Māyā Devī in a dream. The white elephant, therefore, is a sacred symbol with the Buddhists, and is very much respected. This rock-engraving itself is a piece of art: lines show sureness of its execution and a kind of linear movement. The plasticity of the drawing reflects the full vigour of an elephant in its animated walk. It may be mentioned in this connection that the elephants depicted on the tribal coins have, by and large, much more naturalistic appearance than those occurring on the punch-marked silver coins.

Such graphic representation forming part of an inscription has hardly any counterpart in the early period. The introduction of labelled sculptures and reliefs during the second-first centuries BC possibly did not allow the practice to grow. A crude representation of an animal and pot with plants sprouting from the mouth (fig. 23, *1*; pl. XV A) is found in the Shakardarra Kharoshṭhī inscription ascribable to the second-first century (*CII*, II, part I, p. 159). The Rawal spurious inscription of the year 40 (*EI*, XIX, p. 206), being the clumsy copy of the above-mentioned epigraph also contains the same representation. It is difficult to find out its exact significance: the animal seems to be a horse with two spots on the body and a crest-like decoration on the head. If the drawing of the plant has any connection with reality it is more nearer to the palmyra leaves placed inside the pot.

Other animal representations in inscriptions belong to medieval times. The bull in the two inscriptions of Kampana from Madam (*EI*, XXVIII, p. 154), AD 1362-63, may signify the theriomorphic representation of Śiva (fig. 23, *2*). The figures of cow with calf in certain imprecatory scenes along with Śiva-*liṅga* may also have Śaiva association. An interesting example is the scene depicted in the Miraj plates of Śaka year 980 (AD 1058) of Mārasiṁha, the Śilāhāra king (*CII*, VI, pp. 200-206). Side iii of the copper-plate contains a scene (pl. XX) showing a seated figure with folded hands worshipping Śiva-*liṅga* and the bull (Nandi); on the upper portion are engraved the outline of the sun and the moon. Likewise, individual representation of boar (see below pp. 80-81) stands possibly as a Vaishṇava emblem (*EI*, VII, p. 96; XXXV, 136).

2. Fishes

The fish has always been an auspicious symbol in Indian plastic tradition, be it Brahmanical or Buddhist. It is, in fact, one of the ten incarnations of Vishṇu. But fishes have their independent role as well. For example, a pair of fishes are considered as a *maṅgala* sign. In the Indus valley script, fish is an oft-repeated sign; fish also figures in terracotta sealings from Harappan sites as part of a scene. Fish-designs also occur frequently on the punch-marked coins, the commonest type is that representing two or four fishes in an oblong tank. Despite stylized forms, several varieties of fishes are distinguishable on the punch-marked coins. Compared to these forms, those appearing in the inscriptions are quite realistically drawn.

However, their occurrence in the epigraphs is very much limited; not more than half-a-dozen examples have so far come to light. Further, these inscriptions belonging to two different dynasties, come from two different areas, Kathiawar and far south.

The earliest series with fish-impression is confined to Kathiawar and belongs to the Saindhavas of Bhūtāmbilikā; these inscriptions are ascribed to the eighth-ninth centuries. Perhaps, the fish was the emblem of these kings, and it was a kind of marine fish or a shark. These kings claimed to be the masters of the western sea, 'and so must have proudly claimed fish to be their emblem' like the Pāṇḍyas of the extreme south. Generally, the fish is outlined at the conclusion of the copper-plate grants (fig. 17, *2, 3*; pl. XII) (*EI*, XXVI, pp. 185).

The crest of the Pāṇḍya kings is the carp which is engraved not only on their coins but also in some inscriptions. In the Ranganatha inscription of Sundara Pāṇḍya, AD 1250-51 (*EI*, III, p. 7) the inscription is flanked by two fishes of the carp variety (fig. 17, *4, 5*). These fishes are boldly executed and bear the imprint of the scribe's artistic talent. Fish is found inscribed also in an inscription from Nepal (fig. 17, *1*); it occupies the top of the slab above the epigraph.[1]

3. Birds

Birds rarely occur in the inscriptions. In fact, the present collection includes only two examples—one in the Saheth-Maheth plate (see also above, Chapter 7), (fig. 15, *24*) of Govinda Chandra (fig. 18, *4*) (*EI*, XI, p. 20), AD 1128-29 and the other in the Ajayagadh stone inscription of Nana from Bundelkhand, AD 1402-03. What is found at the end of the first-mentioned inscription is something like a bird's wing followed by two vertical strokes and another symbol in the form of the letter *gha*. The Chandella record from Ajayagadh, however, portrays a fine representation of a duck holding a stalk in its beak (fig. 18, *5*) (*EI*, XXVIII, p. 98).

4. Mythical figures

Mythical animals and birds occur quite frequently in the medieval inscriptions. Of the two mythical animals, *iha-mṛiga*, the one in the Akkalapundi grant of Siṅgaya Nāyaka, AD 1368, from district Godavari, Andhra Pradesh (*EI*, XIII, p. 259) bears the representation of a *vyāla* with a leonine appearance (fig. 18, *1*). The Danteswara Sanskrit and Hindi inscriptions of Dikpāladeva, AD 1702, from Jagdalpur, Madhya Pradesh, have also a fanciful animal figure with a tiger-face (fig. 18, *2*); it is inscribed above the Hindi inscription (*EI*, XII, p. 242).

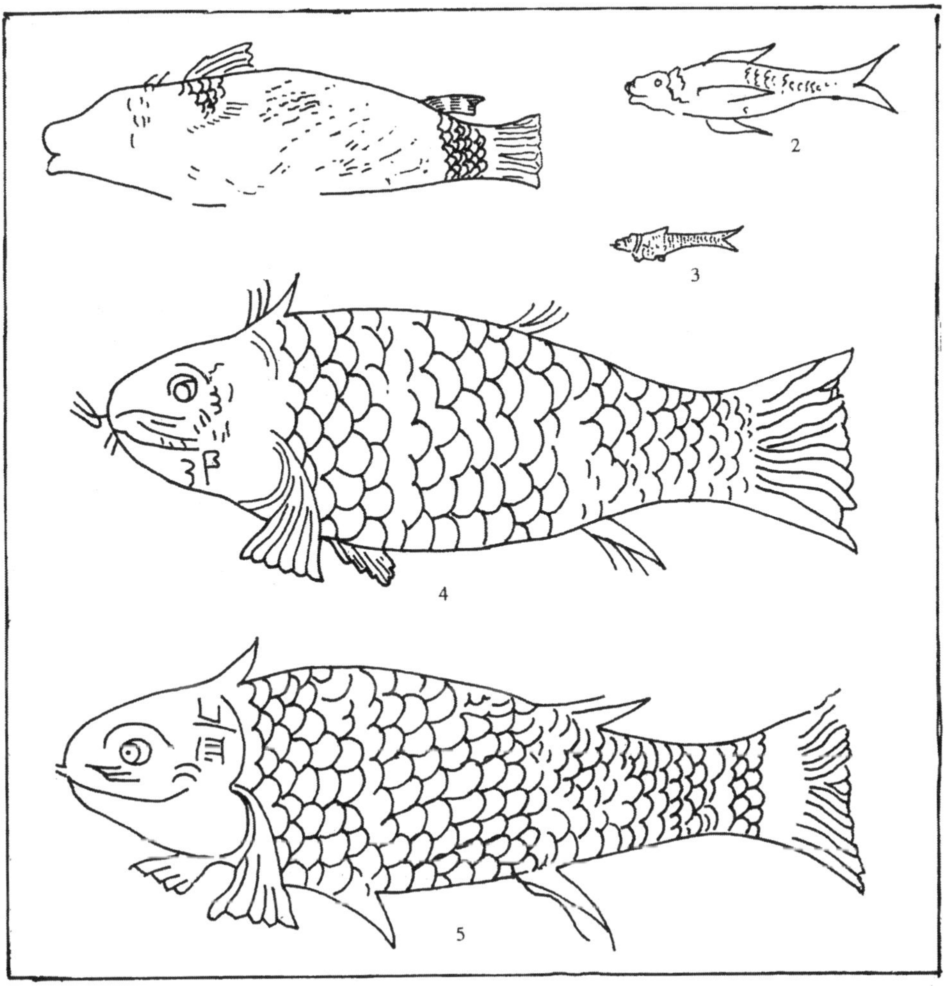

Fig. 17. Fishes: 1 Nepalese inscription; 2 and 3 copper-plate grants of Saindhavas of Bhūtāmbilikā, Gujarat; 4 and 5 Ranganatha inscription of Sundara Pāṇḍya, AD 1250-51

Of the mythical birds, Garuḍa, the vehicle of Vishṇu, is well-represented in medieval records; it is proposed to describe them along with the Vaishṇava deities. In the south, another kind of mythical bird is noticed in the inscription: it is known as *Gaṇḍabheruṇḍa*. The ninth plate of the Pentapadu grant of Choḍa Bhaktirāja, Śaka 1265 (*EI*, XXXIII, p. 219) contains a figure

Fig. 18. Birds and mythical figures: 1 Akkalapundi grant of Siṅgaya Nāyaka, District Godavari, Andhra Pradesh, AD 1368; 2 Dantewara Sanskrit and Hindi inscriptions of Dikpāladeva, from Jagdalpur, Madhya Pradesh, AD 1702; 3 Pentapadu grant of Choḍa Bhaktirāja, Śaka 1265; 4 Saheth-Maheth plate of Govinda Chandra, AD 1128-29; 5 Ajayagadh stone inscription of Nana, Vikrama Saṁvat 1345

standing astride, with two heads of birds facing opposite directions (fig. 18, *3*). The mythical figure holds two elephants by their trunk, one in each hand. There is also an explanatory passage to the left of the figure. It may be mentioned that the donor, Bhaktirāja, enjoyed the title *Gaṇḍabheruṇḍa*. Mostly confined to Andhra, it is noticed in the same form, in the Tripurantakam (district Kurnool) inscription (Śaka 1310) of Annadeva, Vinukonda (district Guntur) inscription (Śaka 1377), etc. (*EI*, XXXIII, p. 219 n.)

5. Religious edifices

The only representation of a religious edifice in an inscription comes from Mahabalipuram (*EI*, X, p. 1), and is dated to the seventh century. At the end of the inscription from Gaṇeśa Ratha is to be seen the representation of the temple (fig. 19, *2*) with the legend *Atyantakāmapallaveśvara griham̐*. The drawing along with the label seems to have been omitted in the duplicate version of the epigraph found at the Dharmarāja *maṇḍapa* (*EI*, X, p. 1).

Some sort of sacrificial altars carved in the middle of the inscription

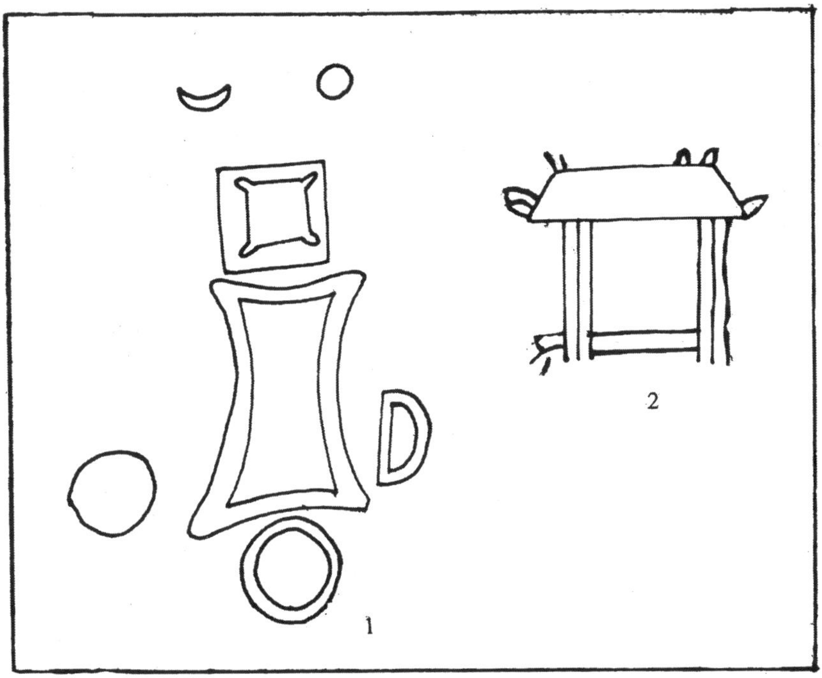

Fig. 19. Religious edifices: 1 sacrificial altar, inscription from Sonda, AD 1674; 2 inscription in Gaṇeśa Ratha, Mahabalipuram, seventh century

from Sonda (*EI*, XXXII, p. 79), AD 1674, may be included here. Four figures, of geometrical types are carved here in relief, and are taken as sacrificial memorial, on the top of the inscription is drawn a crescent and a sun (fig. 19, *1*; pl. X).

6. Human figures

Human figures occurring independently in inscriptions are extremely rare. In the Ajayagadh stone inscription of Nana, AD 1402-03, is to be seen a figure with upraised hands (*EI*, XXVIII, p. 98) (see above, fig. 18, *5*). It is the last of the four symbols appearing in a row in this inscription. An almost full-length view of a human figure dressed in tunic is inscribed in the Mahudi plates of Paramāra Bhoja, AD 1018. Intererestingly enough, the human figure represents Garuḍa, which was the emblem of the Paramāra rulers, (fig. 20, *1*) (*EI*, XXXIII, p. 215).

An interesting example is an early Brāhmī inscription of about first century BC engraved on a slab (pl. XVIII) kept in the Puratattva Sangrahalaya, Jabalpur (*IAR 1964-65*, p. 56, pl. XLVIII). This inscription,

Fig. 20

in Prakrit influenced by Sanskrit, speaks of a certain Vasiṭhiputra Śivaghosha and his minister. On the proper left side of this record is the figure of a person holding a spear in the right hand and reins of two horses in the left hand leading them towards a kind of *yūpa-stambha* by the side of which a *kamaṇḍalu* is depicted. It is not unlikely that the scene is later than the inscription.

7. Gods and goddesses

Figures of gods and goddesses do appear in the inscriptions belonging to the medieval times. The practice seems to have been confined to a few dynastic records, and most likely it was the Paramāras who introduced it some time in the tenth century followed by the Gāhaḍavālas and the Chandelas. In a way, the practice appears to be the culmination of the earlier tradition of carving a wheel in the Gupta records. In some Paramāra records are also found the figures of Garuḍa (*EI*, XIX, p. 236).

(a) *Garuḍa:* The largest number of such representations are those Garuḍa, the mythical bird—the *vāhana* of Vishṇu. It was represented either as royal insignia (*mudrā*), or as royal mark or emblem (*rājāṅka*) in the seals, inscriptions and was also depicted in the sculptures of Vishṇu. The importance of Garuḍa can be seen from the charters of the Gupta ruler Samudragupta and also the reference to Garuḍa in his Allahabad pillar inscription. Similarly, the Garuḍa emblem was depicted on some of the Gupta coins and also found its place as the capital piece of a column (*Garuḍa-dhvaja*).[2] The figure occurs commonly in the Paramāra records of the tenth to the thirteenth century. In fact, Garuḍa was the emblem of the Paramāra rulers, and is generally represented in their copper-plate grants.

These representations covering a period of more than two centuries show the gradual development of the Garuḍa image, and have, therefore, iconographic importance.

The Harsola copper-plate grants of Sīyaka of VS 1005 (AD 949) (*EI*, XIX, p. 236) from district Ahmedabad have, on the corner of the first plate,

←Fig. 20. 1 Mahudi plates of Paramāra Bhoja, Vikrama Saṁvat 1074 (AD 1018); 2 Harsola copper plate grant of (Paramāra) Sīyaka, Vikrama Saṁvat 1005 (AD 949); 3 Grant of Sīyaka, Vikrama Saṁvat 1026 (AD 968); 4 record of Vākpati-Muñja, Vikrama Saṁvat 1038 (AD 981); 5 Mandhata plates of Jayasimhadeva of Dhāra, Saṁvat 1112 (AD 1055-56); 6 Banswara plates of Bhojadeva (Vikrama) Saṁvat 1076 (AD 1020); 7 Bhopal plates of Mahādeva (Vikrama) Saṁvat 1076 (AD 1020); 8 Mehar plate of Dāmodaradeva, Vikrama Saṁvat 1156 (AD 1234); 9 Kadambapadraka grant of Naravarman, AD 1159; 10 Mandhata plates of Devapāla; 11 Mandhata plates of Paramāra Jayasiṁha-Jayavarma, AD 1274

a flying figure of Garuḍa holding a snake in his left arm (fig. 20, *2*). Despite wings at the back, the two-handed figure is more nearer to a human form than to a bird. Such two-armed image of Garuḍa is designated as Tārkshya in the *Śilparatna*. Another grant of Sīyaka (*EI*, XIX, p. 177) has almost a similar representation, (fig. 20, *3*); this record is dated to AD 968 i.e., about twenty years later to the first-mentioned inscription. The records of Vākpati-Muñja, Jayasiṁhadeva and Bhojadeva (*EI*, XXIII, p. 108; III, p. 46; XI, p. 181) contain more or less similar representations (fig. 20, *4-6*). In some cases, however, the snake is held in the palm (*EI*, XI, p. 181 and XXIII, p. 108) (fig. 20, *5-6*). All these figures have almost human appearance though with a beaked nose. The *Vishṇudharmottara* enjoins that Tārkshya should have, among other features, beaked nose like a bird and four arms. But for *Śilparatna* no other texts ascribe snake in Garuḍa's hand. On the other hand, epic and Purāṇic myths are quite emphatic in declaring Garuḍa's association with the snake.

In the Paramāra grants, the representations of Garuḍa follow a uniform iconographic pattern till about the middle of the twelfth century. The Bhopal plates of Mahākumāra Harichaṁdradeva, AD 1157 (*EI*, XXIV, p. 225) do not show any snake and, further, the image is flanked by a pillar on either side (fig. 20, *7*). The Mehar plate of Dāmodaradeva, AD 1234 (*EI*, XXVII, p. 182), has, on the obverse of the seal on the top of the plate, "a figure of Vishṇu either riding on Garuḍa, his traditional vehicle, or in the angry attitude of slaying a fallen foe" (fig. 20, *8*): while, on the reverse, is carved the rayed disc of the sun inside a crescent on a pedestal (see above, p. 64, fig. 15, *25*). On the other hand, the Kadambapadraka grant of Naravarman, AD 1159, reveals the image of Garuḍa with at least four snakes (fig. 20, *9*) (*EI*, XX, p. 105). Again, the Mandhata plates of Devapāla, AD 1225 (*EI*, IX, p. 103) have, in the lower proper right corner of the first side of the third plate, a space marked off by double lines which enclose a figure of Garuḍa with two serpents standing erect on either side (fig. 20, *10*). No snake, however, can be seen on the body or in his arms. The Garuḍa figure at the end of the Mandhata plates of Paramāra Jayasiṁha-Jayavarman, AD 1274 (*EI*, XXXII, p. 139) marks a sharp departure from the earlier examples. Here, Garuḍa is depicted as four-armed without any snake or any other attribute in his hands: his front hands are in *namaskāra-mudrā* while the rear ones in the posture of supporting, as it were, the load of his legs. The image is shown installed inside a structure (fig. 20, *11*).

(b) *Boar incarnation of Vishṇu:* There are two instances of the boar incarnation in the inscriptions. The one engraved on the projection of one of the copper-plate grants from Bihar (fig. 21, *1*) (*EI*, XXXV, p. 136), AD

Fig. 21. Boar incarnation of Vishṇu: 1 copper plate grant from Bihar, AD 1026; 2 Lucknow Museum plate of Kīrtipāla, AD 1111; 3 grant of Prithivīchandra Bhogaśakti from Anjaneri, eighth century

1026, was possibly meant to serve the purpose of the seal. It is not carefully drawn and, as a result, the iconographic features are not very clear. But the Lucknow Museum plate of Kīrtipāla, AD 1111, bears fine representation of the boar incarnation of Vishṇu (*EI*, VII, p. 93). But for the head, the entire body is shown as human (fig. 21, *2*; pl. XIII). The four-armed god is about to tread the snake-hood of Ādiśesha having a coiled body. A flower with its stem intact is touching the neck of the serpent. A tiny figure of a lady seated on his upper left hand represents Bhū-devī or Earth Goddess, and the god is looking at her with loving eyes despite the militant mood. The second side of the plate has representation of *śankha* on the top (pl. XIV). An interesting example of boar is to be seen in the grant of the king Pṛithivīchandra Bhogaśakti, found at Anjanari in Nasik District and datable to the eighth century AD (fig. 21, *3*) (*EI*, XXV, p. 225).

(c) *Gaja-Lakshmī and Lakshmī*: Śrī Lakshmī is the Indian goddess of good luck, prosperity and abundance, and is respected by all religious creeds. As a very early coin-device, the goddess appears in an uninscribed coin from Kausambi, on the coins of Viśākhadeva, Śivadatta and on the uninscribed coins of Ujjayini.[4] Equally old is her occurrence in the sculptures found on the early monuments of central India. But she figures in the inscriptions only during the medieval times, and is confined only to the Chandella records of the twelfth-thirteenth centuries.

The figure occurs in the middle of the first four lines or in the centre; the former seems to be an earlier practice. In the Garra plates of the Chandella Trailokyavarman, AD 1205 (*EI*, XVI, p. 272), the goddess is

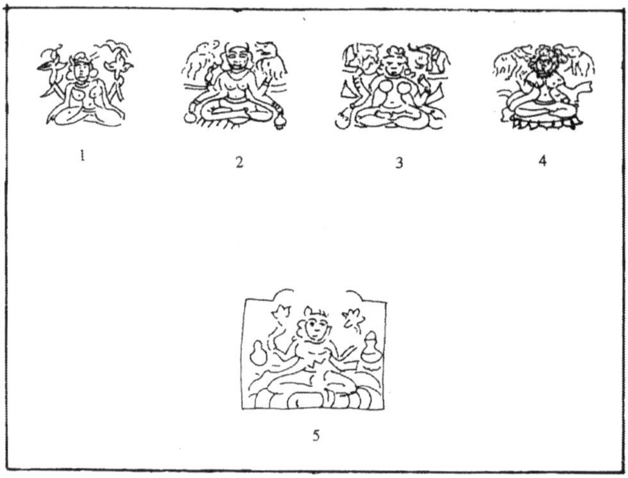

Fig. 22. 1 Garra plates of Chandella Trailokyavarman, AD 1205; 2 Chandella records of Madanavarmadeva; 3 Pachar plate of Paramardideva, AD 1171; 4 Mahoba plates of Paramardideva, AD 1171; 5 Charkhari plates of Hammiradeva, AD 1289

engraved in the centre of each plate (fig. 22, *1*). Perhaps Gaja-Lakshmī is an earlier motif in the Chandella records as the figure appears in the inscriptions of Madanavarmadeva (fig. 22, *2*), Paramardideva and Trailokyavarman (*EI*, XXXII, p. 118): Lakshmī is noticed only in the records of Trailokyavarman and Hammīravarmadeva. In the mode of delineation of these figures both the forms betray common features. Invariably these are seated figures with four arms, two of which hold either lotus buds or full-blossomed lotus flowers. Rarely do these representations reveal any artistic quality.

The goddess Gaja-Lakshmī in the Pachar plate of Paramardideva (*EI*, X, p. 44), AD 1171, has an elephant standing on each side with uplifted trunck apparently to pour water over her head (fig. 22, *3*). In each of her lower hands she holds possibly a pot of nectar (*amritaghaṭa*), the other two hands showing lotus-buds. The figure is nearly the same as that found on the Banda district plate of Madanavarmadeva and resembles the one incised on the first of the Ichchawar plates of Paramardideva and the Semra plates of the same king. In the last mentioned case the goddess is squatting on a lotus-seat (*EI*, IV, p. 153). Likewise, the Mahoba plates of Paramardideva (*EI*, XVI, p. 9), AD 1173, show the goddess on her lotus-seat (fig. 22, *4*), which is absent in the Garra plates of Trailokyavarman, AD 1205 (*EI*, XVI, p. 272). In this example, the goddess Lakshmī has in her upper two hands lotuses while no attributes are to be seen in the lower hands. But the Charkhari plate of Hammīravarmadeva, AD 1289 (*EI*, XX, p. 134) shows the representation of the goddess seated on the lotus with a full-blossomed lotus in each of her upper hands, the lower ones holding pots of nectar (fig. 22, *5*). It is an extremely stylized figure: two upraised hands and the head form, as it were, something like a three-headed symbol simulating either a *śrīvatsa* or *triratna*. This is an example of a figure forming a representation of symbol-cum-image of the goddess Lakshmī or Śrī, the like of which is already described by J.N. Banerjea. Such figures—two from Kaveripakkam and the one from Thanjavur—are in the collection of the Madras Museum; all the three pieces are dated to the early medieval period.[5]

(d) *Śiva-liṅga*: From a very early period the Śaivas in general used to worship emblem of Śiva or Śiva-*liṅga* as the principal object of worship in a temple. Banerjea has shown from archaeological, numismatic and glyptic representations of the emblem that the phallic character of the Śiva worship was prevalent in India from a very remote past.[6] However, such aniconic form appeared in the inscriptions only in the medieval time, that too, generally as a part of the imprecatory scenes. Even the theriomorphic form as an independent motif did not attain any popularity. It was in the Gaya inscription of Govindapāla, AD 1175, (*EI*, XXXV, p. 233) that a Śiva-*liṅga* (fig. 23, *3*) is found engraved on the top of the inscription while a female deity is carved in relief at the end.

8. Imprecatory scenes and sculptural ornamentation

Sometimes inscriptions are inseparably connected with the sculptural ornamentation of the records. Under this class fall the labels to sculptures, inscriptions on the pedestal of images or architectural members, memorial inscriptions and imprecatory scenes. The last two classes have a direct bearing on the contents of their epigraphs. D.C. Sircar writes: "The sculptured representation of one or more hands raised upwards (i.e. pointing to heaven) indicated that the inscriptions in question recorded the commitment of Sati by a lady or several ladies who went to heaven as a result of the meritorious act. Inscriptions recording the deaths of heroes in battle generally bear sculptures depicting a warrior sometimes as dead or as engaged in fighting. In many cases, the *Sati-* and hero-stones bearing such representations do not bear any inscription apparently because the meaning of the representations was easily understood."[7]

Memorial-pillars carved with scenes from the life of the dead also bear inscriptions. The practice assumed wide vogue at Nagarjunakonda during the Ikshvāku period (third-fourth centuries AD).[8] In such pillars sculptural representations are more prominent than the epigraph, which is incised

Fig. 23

generally at the bottom-most panel. In some cases (*EI*, XXX, p. 278) the panel is in the centre: a ninth century inscription from district Chittoor shows a three feet square panel in the centre depicting a warrior wielding a massive sword and holding with his other hand the tuft of his opponent. Two damsels on either side are depicted as if in the act of leading the hero heavenwards. In another class of inscriptions, the reliefs show devotees offering their heads to a deity.[9]

The imprecatory scenes and benedictive figures connected with inscriptions possibly started in the form of sculptural representations. Such examples are common in the Western Chālukyan records from districts Dharwar and Belgaum. However, the Tuppad-Kurhatti inscription of the Rāshṭrakūta king Akālavarsha Krishṇa III, Śaka 868 (AD 945) (*EI*, XIV, p. 364) contains the sculptures of a *liṅga* on a pedestal, a squatting figure in the proper right and a cow with suckling calf. The sun and the moon so frequent in such representations are absent in the record. But the Sogal inscription of the reign of Taila II, AD 980 (*EI*, XVI, p. 1) have sculptures consisting of a shrine, a *liṅga*, with a priest, a squatting bull, a votary and a cow with suckling calf. the sun and the moon. In place of Śiva-*liṅga* sometime squatting Jina is also shown as in the Mulgund inscription of the reign of Someśvara I, Śaka 975 (*EI*, XVI, p. 53). The Managoli inscription of the time of the Kālachurya king Bijjala, AD 1161 (*EI*, V, p. 9), reveals the addition of a few more objects like a crooked sword and dagger or knife. There are instances where only the sun and the moon are engraved; it appears to be a later development, for these inscriptions from Sonda (see above, fig. 19, *1*) are dated to the seventeenth century (*EI*, XXXII, p. 79).

The pattern followed in the sculptural ornamentations is noticeable with slight variations also in the drawings accompanying the records. Such drawings appear to be the creation of the scribes, and not of any sculptors and they must have engraved them with the help of the scribe's tools and implements. One of the earliest such representations comes from the Mindigal inscription of Rājādhirāja, AD 1047-48 (*EI*, V, pp. 205) where, at

← Fig. 23. 1 Shakardarra Kharoshṭhī inscription of the year 40 (second-first century); 2 inscription of Kampana from Taṭākapurīśvara temple at Madan, AD 1362-63; 3 Gaya inscription mentioning Govindapāla, AD 1175; 4 Someśvara temple, Mindigul inscription of Rājādhirāja, Śaka Saṁvat 970 (AD 1047-48); 5 Narayanpal inscription of Guṇḍa Mahādevī, Śaka 1033 (AD 1111); 6 Bitragunta grant of Saṅgama II, early thirteenth century; 7 Jambukeśvaram grant of Vijayaranga Chokkanātha Nāyaka, Śaka 1630; 8 Pushpagiri inscription of the time of Yādava Siṅghana, early thirteenth century; 9 Machupalle inscription of the time of Somadeva-Mahārāja, Śaka 1178 (AD 1255); 10 Anmakonda pillar inscription of Prola, AD 1117

Fig. 24. Imprecatory scenes: 1 Rājapura copper plates of Madhurāntakadeva, Śaka 987; 2 Bodh-Gaya inscription of the time of Aśokachalla-Lakshmaṇa, Saṁvat 74 (AD 1194)

the top, to the proper right of the lines 1 and 2, are engraved the figures of a cow and a calf (fig. 23, *4*; pl. XVI).

The records of the Bastar region in central India introduced a new element in such scenes. The Rajapura copper-plates of Madhurāntakadeva, Śaka 987 (*EI*, IX, p. 174) have, on the second side of the third plate, several benedictive and imprecatory figures, viz., twelve hands in a row at the top beneath which stand to the proper left a cow with a bell attached to her neck, a dagger and a shield, a *liṅga* and a woman followed by a donkey, with the figures of the sun and the moon above (fig. 24, *1*; pl. XV B). At the end of the Narayanpal inscription of queen Guṇḍa-mahādevī, the mother of Someśvaradeva, AD 1111 (*EI*, IX, p. 311) are engraved the sun, the moon, a cow and a calf, a dagger and shield with a *liṅga* (fig. 23, *5*; pl. XVII). The Talale plates of Gaṇḍarāditya, Śaka year 1032 (AD 1110) (*CII*, VI, p. 207) contain "engraving of a cow and its suckling calf, with a double-edged sword in an upright position on one side, the whole surmounted by the figures of the sun and the moon" (pl. XIX). According to V.V. Mirashi "the cow is intended to represent land, the milk the produce of the land, the calf the enjoyer, and the sword the royal power. The sun and the moon denote perpetuity. They seem intended to show that the person who receives land by virtue of the grant is to enjoy it under the authority of the king as long as the sun and the moon endure".

The practice of inscribing similar scenes is observed also in some records from Andhra Pradesh as in the Pushpagiri inscription of the time of Yādava Siṅghana (early thirteenth century) (fig. 23, *8*) (*EI*, XXX, p. 32) and the Machupalle inscription of the time of Yādava Siṅghana (fig. 23, *9*) (EI, *XXVIII*, p. 114). The Anmakonda pillar-inscription of Prola (*EI*, IX, p. 256),

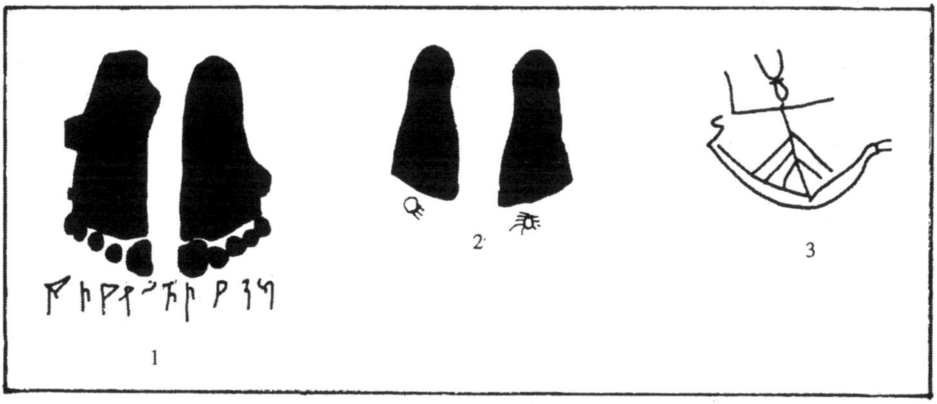

Fig. 25. Graphic representations: 1 Tirath rock-inscription, Swat Valley; 2 Ci-Aruton inscription, Java; 3 Duwe Gala cave inscription, Sri Lanka

AD 1117, at the top of each of the four faces of the pillar is engraved a squatting Jaina ascetic (fig. 23, *10*): on the east face he is flanked by a cow and calf on one side and a dagger and shield on the other, and the north face of the pillar has the representations of the sun and the moon. The Bitragunta grant of Saṅgama II of the Vijayanagara dynasty (*EI*, III, p. 21) bears somewhat different picture: the first side of the first copper-plate has the symbols of the sun and the moon, and below the moon is to be seen the figure of a bull tied by a rope to a tripod surmounted by a trident (fig. 23, *6*). At the top of the Porumamilla tank inscription of Bhāskara Bhavadūr, AD 1369 (*EI*, XIV, p. 97) are incised the figures of Vighṇeśvara with his vehicle, the mouse, the *liṅga*, the sun and the moon. The Jambukesvaram grant of Vijayaraṅga Chokkanātha Nāyaka, Śaka 1630 (*EI*, XVI, p. 88) has the figures of the sun and the moon, a tree, a devotee, a *liṅga*, an elephant and a standing female deity (fig. 23, *7*). It appears that with the advancement of time the scenes became more and more elaborate in certain cases, while the process of simplification was afoot simultaneously. The latter aspect is best exemplified in the Kalyana inscription of Sultān Muhammad, AD 1326 (*EI*, XXXII, p. 165).

These ornamentations are mostly picture imprecations and possess symbolic meaning. According to Hira Lal (*EI*, IX, p. 175), the figures in the Rajapura copper-plates of Madhurāntakadeva (see above p. 85) may be interpreted as follows: "The hands are uplifted, appearently as an expression of benediction on the donor, and they are twelve, probably because there are 12 *pātras* or donees referred to in the inscription. The cow is apparently drawn to remind us that whosoever appropriates the gifted land, will have to reap the same consequences which a cow's curse can produce, or will fall into the same calamity as a cow is in when deprived of her calf. Śiva is shown as the protector against aggression on the spiritual side, and the ruling king's dagger and shield on the temporal. The sun and the moon indicate that the grant is to last as long as these luminaries endure. Lastly the obscene figure of an ass associating with a woman is a vulgar imprecation implying that the transgressor of a gift should be so low-born".

The vulgar imprecation referred to above is a widespread motif and is found engraved, generally at the end of the inscriptions from Karnataka, Madhya Pradesh and Orissa. The Sena kings of Bengal possibly imported the idea in eastern India as is evident from a Bodh-Gaya inscription of Lakshmaṇasena (*EI*, XII, p. 27): at the end of the plate is incised an indecent figure of an ass associating with a pig (fig. 24, 2). The explanation of this scene also occurring in the Kuruspal inscription is given in the same epigraph: *Jo (yo) anyathā karoti tasya pitā gardabhaḥ śūkarī mātā.*

9. Miscellaneous representations

It is not always easy to distinguish a conventionalized form of symbol from naturalistic ones. Flowers, for instance, may be brought under both the categories; similar is the case with wheel or *śaṅkha*. But as these symbols are very popular on the ancient coins they have been included in the group of conventional types. Sometimes, one comes across the picture of a pair of foot-prints in sculptures and paintings. They hardly show any naturalistic outline, yet none can dispute their identification as foot-prints. In Indian inscriptions there are a few examples of such representations which are discussed in this section. For example, a pair of feet or *pādukas* carved on rock or boulder in the Tirath rock-inscription (fig. 25, *1*; pl. XI B) in the Swat valley have the label *Bodhàsa Śakamuṇisā padāṇi* in Kharoshṭhī (*CII*, II, Part (i), p. 8). This reminds one of the foot-prints found in association with some minor rock-edicts of Aśoka. The one found above the edict at Palkigundu is, however, taken to be later in date than the epigraph proper.[10] But the discovery of a pair of foot-prints on a boulder near the newly-discovered Delhi minor rock-edict[11] may make one wonder as to their contemporaneity with the Aśokan inscription. Another interesting example of the depiction of foot-prints is from Ci-Aruton, Java, alongside an inscription in box-headed letters of the Vākāṭaka type and in shell-characters (*EI*, XXII, p. 4). These foot-prints are referred to in the inscription as *Vishṇoriva pādadvayaṁ*, i.e., a pair of foot-prints of Vishṇu (fig. 25, *2*).

As stated above, flowers have been included in the category of conventionalized forms of symbol. But there is one example in a Nepalese inscription which deserves inclusion as a graphic representation (fig. 26).

Fig. 26. Nepal, lotus drawn in an inscription

It is a full-bloom lotus drawn realistically along with its leaves and buds.[12] Mention may be made of a representation of a ship (fig. 25, *3*) at the right side of the Duwe Gala Cave inscription, no. 7, from Sri Lanka[13] datable to about the first century BC.

The authors are conscious of the fact that many more examples of graphic representations have been left out. But sometimes bad impressions or lack of illustrations or impressions of the inscriptions have forced them to leave out several specimens. It is, however, felt that the authors have been able to place before the scholars representative collection of forms and figures, and that the present work may provide a reasonable basis for a still fuller study of this long-neglected subject of Indian epigraphy.

Notes and References

1. Pandit Bhagvanlal Indraji, *Twenty-three Inscriptions from Nepal* (Bombay, 1885), pp. 9-11. Ins. no. 9.
2. J.N. Banerjea, *The Development of Hindu Iconography* (Calcutta, 1956), pp. 10 and 531
3. *Ibid.*, p. 11.
4. *Ibid.*, pp. 110-11.
5. *Ibid.*, p. 376.
6. *Ibid.*, p. 455.
7. D.C. Sircar, *Indian Epigraphy*, p. 89.
8. H. Sarkar and B.N. Mishra, *Nagarjunakoṇḍa* (New Delhi, 1966), p. 43.
9. D.C. Sircar, *op.cit.*, p. 89.
10. R.L. Turner, *The Gavīmaṭh and Pālkiguṇḍu Inscriptions of Aśoka*, Hyderabad Archaeological Series, No. 10 (Hyderabad, 1952), p. 19, pl. IV.
11. M.C. Joshi and B.M. Pande, 'A newly discovered inscription of Aśoka at Bahapur, Delhi,' *Journal of the Royal Asiatic Society of Great Britain & Ireland*, Parts 3 & 4 (1967), pp. 96-98. The pair of foot-prints, on a boulder

near the find-spot of the minor rock edict, has, however not been referred to in the paper cited.

12. Bhagwanlal Indraji, *op.cit.*, Ins. No. 15, p. 16. pl. facing p. 16.
13. D.C. Sircar, *Select Inscriptions bearing on Indian History and Civilization* (Calcutta, 1965), p. 42, pl. XLIII. Examples of ship are not wanting from India. For instance, ship has been shown on a seal from Mohenjo-daro [E.J.H. Mackay, *Further Excavations at Mohenjo-daro* (Delhi, 1938), vol. II, pl. LXXXIX, A]; it also occurs as a motif on a Punch-marked silver coin [Chittaranjan Roy Choudhary, *A Catalogue of Early Indian Coins in the Asutosh Museum*] (Calcutta, 1962), Part I, plate III, 1). Likewise, there are instances of the ship or boat occurring as a motif on the beads from ancient Crete; V.E.G. Kenna, *Cretan Seals* (Oxford, 1960), K 55; fig. 55 Middle Minoan signet from Mochlos; pl. 3, nos. 55, 49, 50.

CHAPTER 9

EPILOGUE

Symbols and graphic representations in Indian Inscriptions show, on the whole, a pattern of development. With their beginnings going back to the Aśokan time, these reflect clearly two different trends: symbols with really abstract forms and those with more or less naturalistic appearance. The latter's growth appears to be quite sporadic till about the Gupta period when the conventionalized forms start yielding place to the other variety. Yet the rise of naturalistic symbols could by no means oust completely the conventionalized ones. It, too, had its continuity and continues till today.

Threads of these very trends are noticeable not only in inscriptions but also on coins. The conventionalized symbols more or less predominate the coin-devices on the punch-marked series, while designs on tribal coins show a blend of the earlier tradition with more naturalistic forms. Emergence of the latter cannot be dated precisely; possibly, this tradition appeared with the introduction of new ideas in the wake of the Indo-Greek and the Kushāṇa rule. During Gupta period this very trend cast its influence in the sphere of inscriptions as well. The use of symbolic wheel and flower in the Gupta and Vākāṭaka records was the outcome of the changed circumstances. Now the apparent meaning of the symbols can easily be understood; one can even find out its inner meaning—its meaning as a cult symbol. As the religious belief of the Gupta monarchs is known, one may easily identify the wheel as the sacred *chakra* of Vishṇu. One also finds a change even in the position of a symbol: it is placed sometime in the centre of the first few lines—a practice followed also by the Chandellas in inscribing the figure of Lakshmī.

The use of conventionalized symbols also did not follow a set track. In fact, there is hardly any symbol enjoying popularity for a very long time. The taurine, the triskelion and the ogee *svastika* of the Aśokan inscriptions were replaced by a number of new symbols in cave-inscriptions from western

India. Again, in subsequent periods, all these forms lost their popularity, some of them being completely forgotten. Only two symbols, *svastika* and the *triratna*, had a somewhat longer lease of life. These two forms had attained religious significance, and hence, survived for a long time, at least as a favourite art-motif. It may be recalled here that despite its remote origin, the equal-limbed *svastika* appeared in inscriptions only during the second-first centuries BC, whereas it occurs on coins in the period of uninscribed cast copper issues. But its ogee variety, which we first find in the Shahi Tump and the Painted Grey Ware (PGW) Cultures, reappears in the Aśokan inscriptions. Surprisingly, ogee *svastika* is extremely rare in the cave-inscriptions in spite of the fact that several examples of equal-limbed variety are represented there. The former variety also occurs on the punch-marked and uninscribed cast copper coins, and several instances of such a *svastika* are to be noticed in the sculptures from Amaravati and Nagarjunakonda.

No less interesting is the history of the *triratna* symbol or its Brahmanical counterpart *śrīvatsa*. In the inscriptions, it appears in the period of Khāravela, sometime in the first century BC and is common in the cave-inscriptions from western India. It also occurs on the punch-marked or on the cast copper coins. Forms noticed in western Indian cave-inscriptions hardly reveal any uniformity, thereby suggesting that its emergence then was a recent event. Numerous other symbols like altar, *ḍamaru*, etc., might also have come into existence in the same period. These symbols, on the whole appear to be local in character, and might have been introduced by a distinct group of people with intimate knowledge of distant lands, for many of these forms do not seen to be present in the entire gamut of Indian symbolism. Even it is not unlikely that the structure of *triratna* symbol got mixed up with the idea of scarab, the sacred beetle of ancient Egypt. Some of the western Indian examples bear some similarity with the four-winged beetles represented on the seals and stamps from Egypt and Palestine.[1] The presence of tentacle like objects in some representations from the western Indian caves is also noteworthy. Mention has already been made about the representation of a beetle approaching a flower, a favourite design on the punch-marked silver coins (p. 55). But as a developed art-motif *triratna* symbol is found as early as the second century BC in the art of Bharhut.[2]

Observations made so far seem to have some bearing on the chronology of some of the series of coins in ancient India. As stated above, *triratna* appear either on the punch-marked or the uninscribed cast copper coins. On the basis of the Hathigumpha and cave-inscriptions one may possibly date the coin-series with *triratna* to the second-first centuries BC. This was also the period when the triangular-headed standard within railing—a device occurring in the Hathigumpha inscription and on some tribal coins—came into vogue.

Again, on the basis of the symbols in inscriptions one may also say that the coins with hill surmounted by crescent, tree with three leaves and *svastika* might have been issued some time in the third century BC. The last two symbols are practically absent in the punch-marked silver issues but they occur on the uninscribed cast copper coins. In all likelihood, the hill surmounted by a crescent is also a late device as it is absent in the Golakhpur hoard generally ascribed to the early series of punch-marked silver coins.[3] This symbol is engraved in the Sohagaura copper-plate along with a tree having only three leaves. All this may suggest that the uninscribed cast copper coins might not have been issued much earlier than the Aśokan and the Sohagaura inscriptions. To postulate that they predated the punch-marked silver coins is to disregard the chain of continuity that exists between the cast copper coins and the tribal series of Allan. If the above suggestion regarding the date of uninscribed cast copper coins is accepted one may, then, assume the latter as the junior contemporary of the punch-marked silver coins.

An intimate connection in the use of symbols seem to have existed between the early issues of coins and the inscriptions. Of course, from the time of the Indo-Greeks, Kushāṇs and some tribal republics, naturalistic representation became common in numismatic tradition. This influence spread gradually to the domain of symbolism in inscriptions but the older tradition of symbolic forms continued alongside the other. The floral design started in the Vākāṭaka records, and was soon transformed into formal conventionalized or geometrical devices. In fact, such floral ornamentation, apart from the use of *siddhaṁ* or *Oṁ* symbols, assumed wide currency in the medieval period when use of old symbols seems to have been rarely made. Evidently, the pattern of symbolism and the idea associated with its use might have undergone some change. At that time flowers, *śaṅkha, mañjarī, chakra*, fish, circle, criss-cross and intertwined designs received prominence over *svastika*, *triratna* and other early symbols. Some elementary forms are comparable with those noticed on the early coins but such similarity does not necessarily signify commonness of ideas. Ideas behind the symbols change with time, change with the rise of new myths and legends. Further, the types of symbols do not also remain constant: in fact, each age has its own sets of symbols.

It also appears that each class of symbolism has its own characteristic forms. Indeed there might not have been any common fund of symbols from which different series could derive or select theirs. A few symbols, mostly well-known ones, might have been commonly shared by different classes, but once the entire collection is taken into account the similarity appears more apparent than real. Take for instance, mason's marks: they are so unlike the symbols used on coins or in inscriptions. Likewise tattoo-marks look, as it were, belonging to an altogether different sphere. Again, if one compares the symbols on the punch-marked coins with the graffiti on pottery the conclusion becomes apparent. Even at the risk of digression it is proposed to deal with this aspect at some length.

B.B. Lal[4] has catalogued thirty-one graffiti from the Harappan pottery compared to thirty-seven of the chalcolithic period and forty-nine of the megalithic culture. Obviously, each phase was responsible for introducing new forms, although older ones had their continuity too. The number of exclusively chalcolithic and megalithic graffiti is twenty-three and six respectively. Thus chalcolithic people must have added considerably to the stock of existing graffiti-marks. Despite the fact that all the Harappan graffiti continued in the megalithic, only seventeen are common between the Harappan and the chalcolithic; fifteen symbols, however, were not at all taken over by the latter. Similarly, only twelve graffiti are common between the chalcolithic and the megalithic, and about eleven symbols were not used by the megalithic-using people. It clearly shows that certain forms continued for a long time in spite of the emergence of new ones. This increase in the number of symbols in each period may be explained in two ways; it might have been due to the arrival of new people with a different culture and a new outlook, or for the creation of new myths giving birth to new visual forms. The chalcolithic people introduced certain new symbols including different kinds of noose and knot designs.

The same process continued even in later times. Of more than two hundred symbols on the punch-marked catalogued by Allan, only twenty-four have their moorings in the earlier tradition of graffiti marks. A vast number of coin-devices were, therefore, evolved or introduced during the period of punch-marked coins. This might have taken place at the beginning of the sixth century BC. when India had established intimate contact with the outside world. Moreover, the creation of the Brahmanic literature with the supplementary Upanishads, possibly released a flood of myths stirring popular imagination. The development of new symbols out of oral or written tradition was not, therefore, wholly responsible for the sudden emergence of galaxy of coin-devices.

Symbols used in inscriptions also show evidence of new arrivals; only about a dozen examples are common between coins and inscriptions. In cave-inscriptions of western India alone there are about ten types, which have earlier parallels; many of them do not continue even for a short period of time.

That a marked dissimilarity exists between different classes of symbols may be taken as a reasonable hypothesis. At the same time, one cannot also deny certain elements of commonness amongst divergent groups; and this may be the result of their being within the bounds of the same time time and space. Of the ancient mason's marks collected so far only about a dozen exhibit forms similar to those of the graffiti marks, while about a dozen and a half of the modern tattoo-marks are comparable to the graffiti on ancient pottery.

Here it is necessary to sound a word of caution. All these comparative statements are practically based on insufficient data for there is hardly any comprehensive survey in India on mason's marks and tattoo-decorations. Further, the purpose of using symbols in different spheres is not very clear as yet because the meaning and significance of symbols cannot be comprehended with any amount of certainty. In the available studies on symbolism in India emphasis has hardly been laid on the inner meaning of the symbols; as a result nothing beyond the apparent meaning is known. In the circumstances, it is not possible to throw any light on the probable causes of dissimilarities amongst various classes of symbols. It is interesting to note that each tattoo-mark has a name, and could therefore be of some help in determining the meaning of comparable symbols and other classes.

It is, however, fairly certain that symbols in inscriptions are auspicious marks or *maṅgalas*, the invocation of which bring good luck and success. Perhaps these are sacred marks invested with magical properties. The reason for considering them so is not always easy. On the basis of the present-day usage, textual references on rites and rituals, one may interpret a large number of symbols as auspicious, sacred or magico-religious in character. Yet several others may defy an attempt to decipher them because of the absence of textual references or modern usage. In some instances tribal rites, customs and belief in totem are likely to throw light on the nature of symbols. A few examples to substantiate this point of view may be cited here. Thus, the sanctity of frogs, sometimes depicted on the punch-marked coins may be adduced not only from the story of frog-maiden in the *Mahābhārata* but also from the worship of the frog (not as totem) in Ayodhya region and Nepal.[5] A dog-like animal shown on a hill in certain devices on the punch-marked coins may be taken as the hound guarding the path to the heaven.[6] The tortoise and the fish are possibly *avatāras* of Vishṇu: the fish within an oblong or semi-circular enclosure may also remind one of the flood narrated in the *Śatapatha Brāhmaṇa*. Such instances can be multiplied but that would be a long digression. The issue in hand is to indicate that symbols—each one with a mythic or ritualistic background—are representations of objects of sanctity and auspiciousness.

Even today an ordinary letter or a document starts with an auspicious sign or *svasti-vāchana* like *Oṁ, Śrī Śrī* etc., expressed in words or in symbols. In ancient times, the practice must have been widespread. On this analogy, the symbols used in the inscriptions may also be taken as auspicious marks. While describing the individual symbols, an attempt has been made as far as possible to bring out this aspect. But when the symbols are used collectively do they signify the same character? Those used in pairs as one finds in the Hathigumpha and in some cave-inscriptions from western India may have the same purpose. Yet to compare in like manner the groups of seven or four symbols in a row noticed in the Sohagaura and Kailvan inscriptions is difficult. Such collective occurrence could be compared with those on the punch-marked coins: however, in the present state of our knowledge it is difficult for us to hazard a guess about their meaning and purpose. It is worth noting that both these epigraphs contain realistic representations alongside the conventionalized forms. The contents of the Sohagaura inscription seem to have some bearing on the representation of the symbols; at least the two granaries mentioned in the text may be identified with the ones depicted therein. Similarly the symbols in the Kailvan inscription may have a direct relation with the funerary nature of the epigraph. The narrow-necked pitcher, sacrificial or cooking stick and the *ḍamaru* might stand for the articles used by the dead during his life-time. But the significance of the double *svastika* is not known although it may well be the teacher's object of meditation or a *chiti* for sacrifice. One of the *svastikas* touches the stick possibly indicating its use as a stick connected with sacrifice.

Enough has been written regarding the identification of the symbols in the Sohagaura copper-plate. Suffice it to say here that the symbols, like the nature of the epigraph, are expected to reveal the character of a royal proclamation. The hill surmounted by a crescent appears to be royal insignia. It is followed by a long spear with a leaf-shaped blade symbolizing the regal authority which would protect the granaries. The two trees depicted in the plate do not seem to be ordinary ones, be it a leafsome or leafless. As they have railings around them they may be taken as sacred trees—*vrikshachaitya*. Following Eliade, such a tree may also be identified as Cosmic Tree which upholds the three worlds upon one axis.[7] Its branches reach heaven while the roots plunge into hell. The three leaves of the first tree possibly proclaim this very fact explicitly. Again, the railed second tree has at its uppermost point a fork-like terminal simulating a bird with its wings spread: it may remind one of the passage in the *Taittirīya Saṁhitā* (I. 7. 9) wherein the climber of a ceremonial tree is compared with a bird. Anyway, these are sacred trees, the *chaityas* portrayed as sentinel of the heavenly protector. One may, then, take this group of symbols as representing both heavenly and earthly protectors of the granaries shown, as it were, located near the sacred *chaityas*.

Like the Cosmic Tree, the hill is also considered by Eliade as a symbolism of the 'centre'. "This symbol of a Mountain, a Tree or a Column situated at the Centre of the World is extremely widely distributed. We may recall the Mount Meru of Indian tradition, Haraberezaiti of the Iranians, the Norse Himingbjör, the "Mount of the Lands" in the Mesopotamian tradition, Mount Tabor in Palestine (which may signify *tabbur*—that is, "navel" or *omphalos*). Mount Gerizim, again in Palestine, which is expressly named the "navel of the earth," and Golgotha which, for Christians, represented the centre of the world, etc."[8] Such hills are considered sacred—a sacred spot, a point of intersection of Heaven, Earth and Hell. Their highest points touch Heaven, here indicated by a crescent. In protohistoric cultures of India, such hill-symbols are entirely absent. On the other hand, it is not a symbol exclusive to Indian symbolism:[9] perhaps it might have spread to India in early historical period—may be during the fourth-third centuries BC.

In course of time other types of symbolism of centre replaced tree, hill, ladder or bridge symbols.[10] For example, circle with a dot, floral symbol invariably with a centre in the form of a circle—all of them having their origin in a very early period—are expressions of mature philosophical speculations connected with the symbolism of the centre. The world is often conceived as a lotus-flower, and circle as representing the cosmos. Eight pellets around a central dot may stand for *navagraha* or nine planets. Such symbol began appearing in inscriptions from the fifth century although its popularity reached heights only during the medieval period.

The union of *purusha* and *prakriti*, female force with the male, is another favourite theme in Indian philosophy from a very early period, and a great many symbolism may have emerged out of it.

Triangles symbolize female force and interpenetrating triangles union; likewise, concentric circles and flowers may indicate the same. Thus, here is a case of same forms revealing different sides. Symbols may remain the same but they can be utilized as vehicles for conveying different attitude, different philosophy. The converse is also true; the same ideas can be expressed through different symbols.

It is, therefore, obvious that symbols cannot be studied without reference to the context. The fixing up of chronological and geographical horizons is the primary desideratum of the study of symbols, for that alone would provide clues to the prevailing culural, philosophical and mythical backgrounds of the time responsible for giving rise to symbols and images.

As a matter of fact, once symbols are placed in the correct perspective, one can have a better realization of the philosophy of culture of a period—the ethos of the time.

Notes and References

1. P.S.P. Handcock, *Archaeology of the Holy Land* (London, 1916), p. 290, fig. 88, Nos. 9-11.
2. Alexander Cunningham, *The Stupa of Bharhut* (London, 1879), pls. VI, XIII, XXIX and XLVII.
3. E.H.C. Walsh, 'An Examination of a Find of Punch-marked coins in Patna City, with Reference to the Subject of Punch-marked coins Generally,' *Journal of the Bihar and Orissa Research Society*, Vol. V, Part I (1919), pp. 16-72.
4. B.B. Lal, 'From the Megalithic to the Harappa: tracing back the graffiti on the pottery', *Ancient India*, No. 16 (1960), pp. 4-24.
5. E.W. Hopkins, *The Religions of India* (Boston, 1895), p. 536.
6. *Ibid.*, p. 132.
7. Mircea Eliade, *Images and Symbols* (London, 1961), p. 44.
8. Eliade, *ibid.*, p. 42.
9. Ananda K. Coomaraswamy, *History of Indian and Indonesian Art* (London, 1927), p. 44. He writes, "The mountain represented by "arches" (peaks) is found in Mesopotamia and throughout the ancient world, as well as later Indian and Central Asian and Chinese Art".
10. Such symbols occur on the punch-marked and cast copper coins.

CHART

Depicting
Symbols and Graphic Representations in Indian Inscriptions and their Parallels

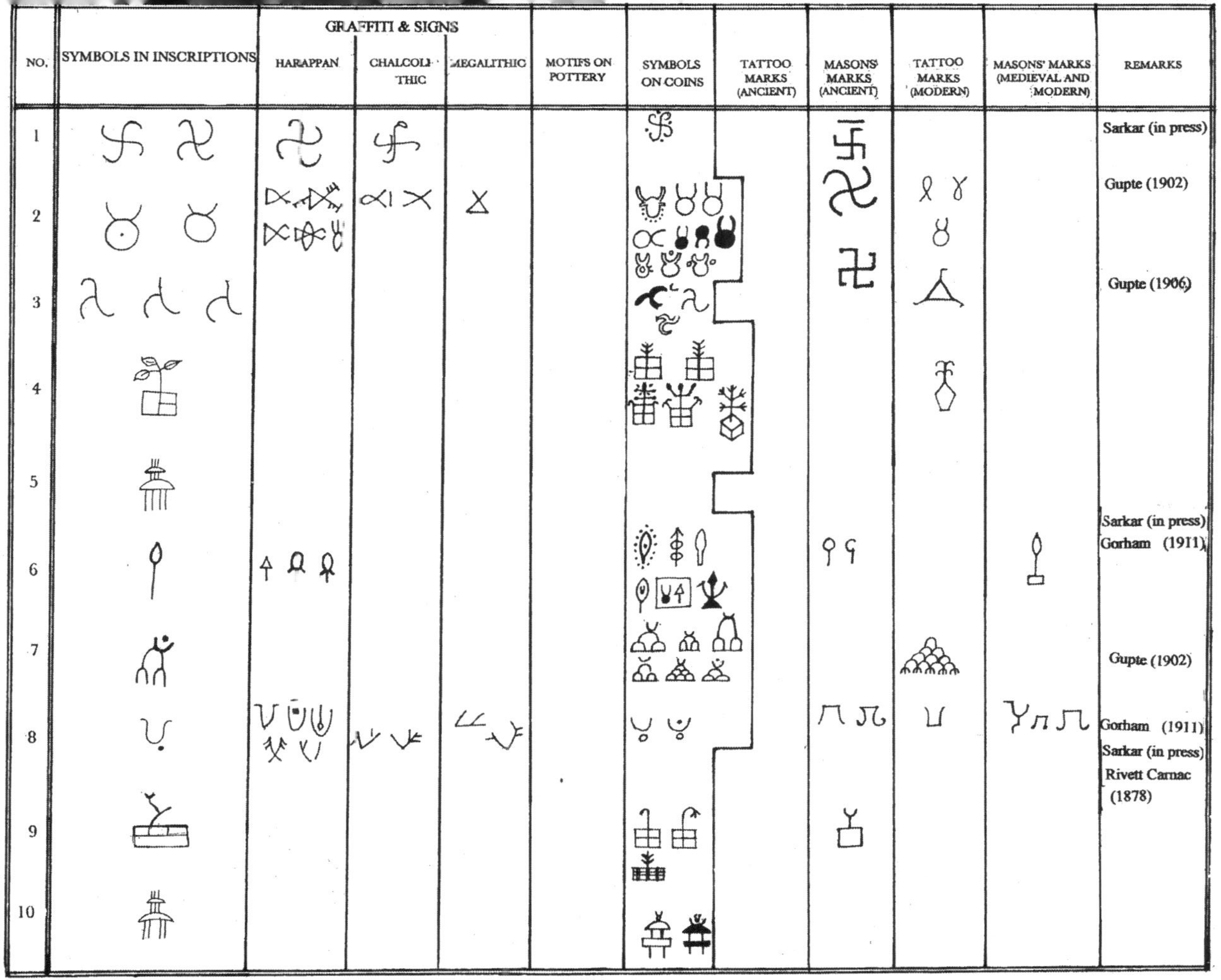

NO.
SYMBOLS IN INSCRIPTIONS
GRAFFITI & SIGNS
HARAPPAN
CHALCOLI- THIC
MEGALITHIC
MOTIFS ON POTTERY
SYMBOLS ON COINS
TATTOO MARKS (ANCIENT)
MASONS' MARKS (ANCIENT)
TATTOO MARKS (MODERN)
MASONS' MARKS (MEDIEVAL AND MODERN)
REMARKS
1
2
3
4
5
6
7
8
9
10
Sarkar (in press)
Gupte (1902)
Gupte (1906)
Sarkar (in press)
Gorham (1911)
Gupte (1902)
Gorham (1911)
Sarkar (in press)
Rivett Carnac (1878)

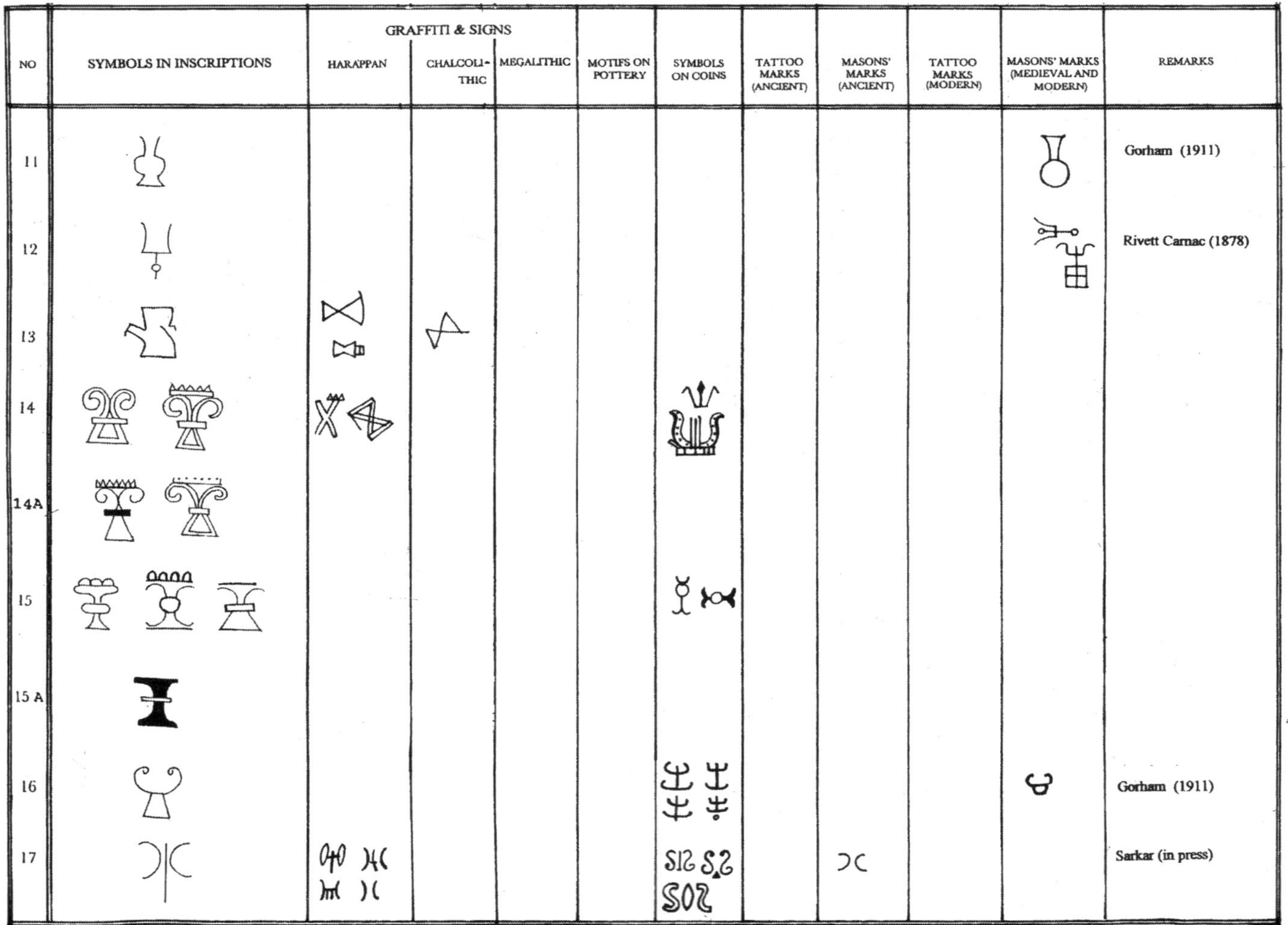

NO	SYMBOLS IN INSCRIPTIONS	GRAFFITI & SIGNS			MOTIFS ON POTTERY	SYMBOLS ON COINS	TATTOO MARKS (ANCIENT)	MASONS' MARKS (ANCIENT)	TATTOO MARKS (MODERN)	MASONS' MARKS (MEDIEVAL AND MODERN)	REMARKS
		HARAPPAN	CHALCOLI-THIC	MEGALITHIC							
11											Gorham (1911)
12											Rivett Carnac (1878)
13											
14											
14A											
15											
15 A											
16											Gorham (1911)
17											Sarkar (in press)

NO	SYMBOLS IN INSCRIPTIONS	GRAFFITI & SIGNS			MOTIFS ON POTTERY	SYMBOLS ON COINS	TATTOO MARKS (ANCIENT)	MASONS' MARKS (ANCIENT)	TATTOO MARKS (MODERN)	MASONS' MARKS (MEDIEVAL AND MODERN)	REMARKS
		HARAPPAN	CHALCOLITHIC	MEGALITHIC							
18											
19											
20											
21											
22											Gorham (1911) Gupte (1902)
23											Cunningham (1879)
24											Sarkar (in press) Gorham (1911)
25											

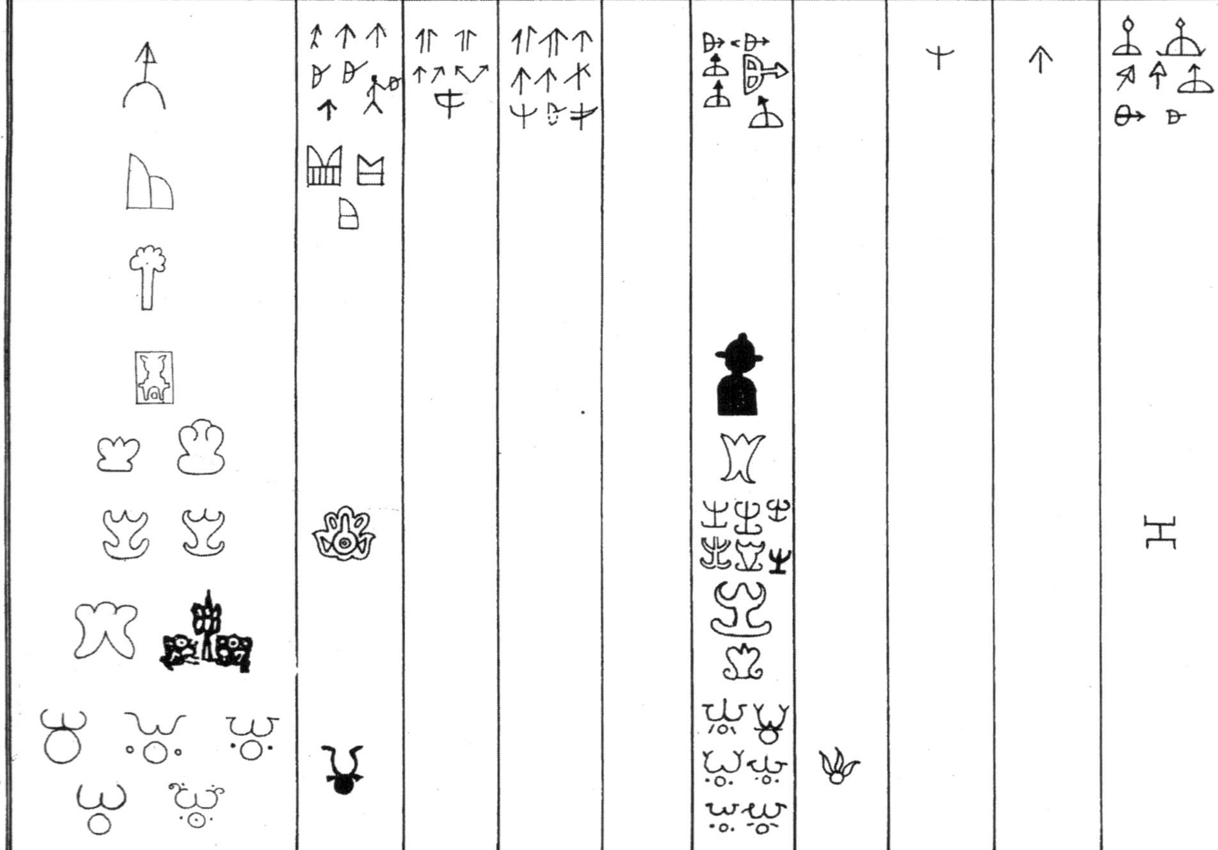

NO	SYMBOLS IN INSCRIPTIONS	GRAFFITI & SIGNS: HARAPPAN	GRAFFITI & SIGNS: CHALCOLITHIC	GRAFFITI & SIGNS: MEGALITHIC	MOTIFS ON POTTERY	SYMBOLS ON COINS	TATTOO MARKS (ANCIENT)	MASONS' MARKS (ANCIENT)	TATTOO MARKS (MODERN)	MASONS' MARKS (MEDIEVAL AND MODERN)	REMARKS
26											Gupte (1902) Rivett Carnac (1878) Gorham (1911)
27											
28											
29											
30											
31											Rivett Carnac (1878)
32											
33											Cunningham (1879)

NC	SYMBOLS IN INSCRIPTIONS	GRAFFITI & SIGNS HARAPPAN	CHALCOLI-THIC	MEGALITHIC	MOTIFS ON POTTERY	SYMBOLS ON COINS	TATTOO MARKS (ANCIENT)	MASONS' MARKS (ANCIENT)	TATTOO MARKS (MODERN)	MASONS' MARKS (MEDIEVAL AND MODERN)	REMARKS
33A											
33B						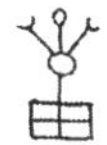					
33C											
34		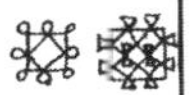									
35											
36					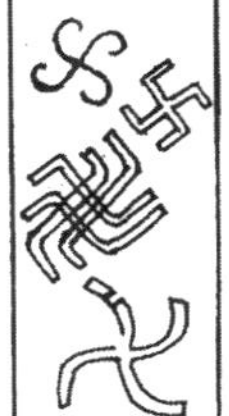	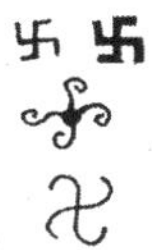			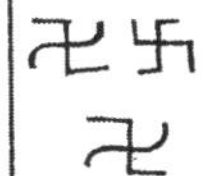		Gupte (1906) Gorham (1911)
36 A	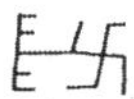										Sarkar (in press)

NO	SYMBOLS IN INSCRIPTIONS	GRAFFITI & SIGNS: HARAPPAN	GRAFFITI & SIGNS: CHALCOLITHIC	GRAFFITI & SIGNS: MEGALITHIC	MOTIFS ON POTTERY	SYMBOLS ON COINS	TATTOO MARKS (ANCIENT)	MASONS' MARKS (ANCIENT)	TATTOO MARKS (MODERN)	MASONS' MARKS (MEDIEVAL AND MODERN)	REMARKS
37		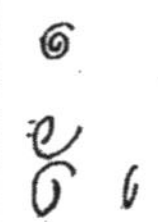									
38		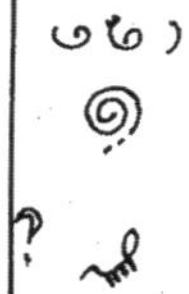									Rivett Carnac (1878)
39	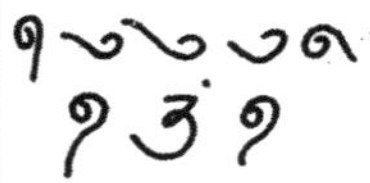										
40	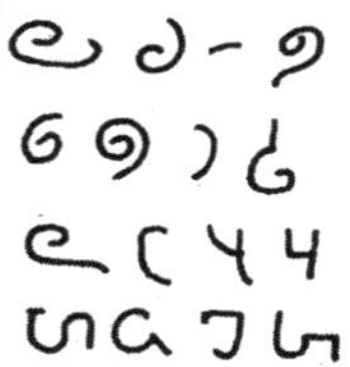	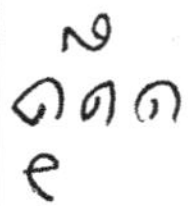								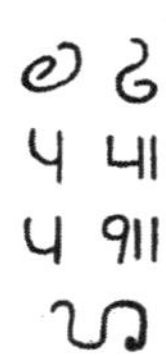	Gorham (1911)

NO	SYMBOLS IN INSCRIPTIONS	GRAFFITI & SIGNS HARAPPAN	CHALCOLITHIC	MEGALITHIC	MOTIFS ON POTTERY	SYMBOLS ON COINS	TATTOO MARKS (ANCIENT)	MASONS' MARKS (ANCIENT)	TATTOO MARKS (MODERN)	MASONS' MARKS (MEDIEVAL AND MODERN)	REMARKS
41											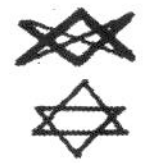 Cunningham (1879)

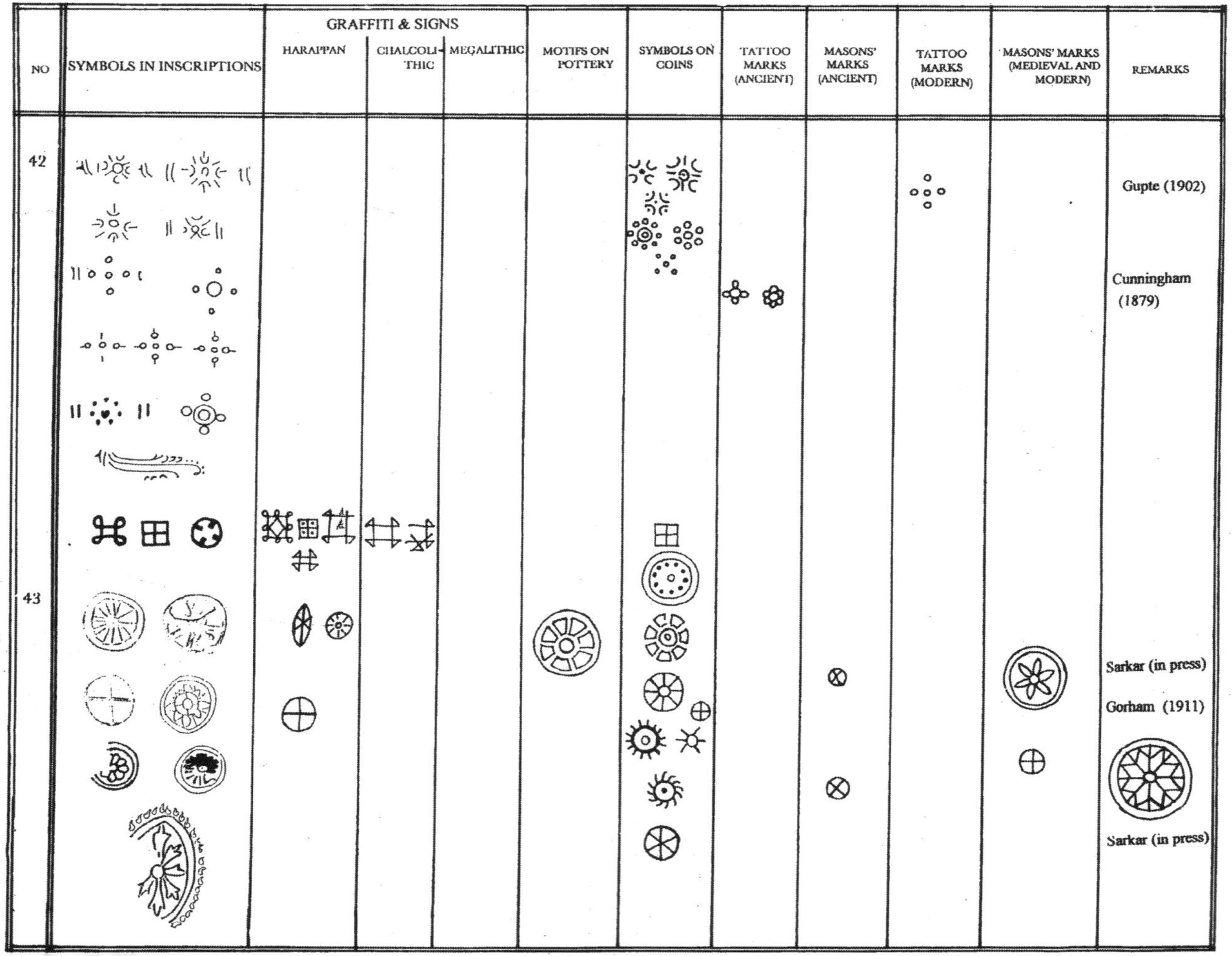
GRAFFITI & SIGNS
NO
SYMBOLS IN INSCRIPTIONS
HARAPPAN
CHALCOLITHIC
MEGALITHIC
MOTIFS ON POTTERY
SYMBOLS ON COINS
TATTOO MARKS (ANCIENT)
MASONS' MARKS (ANCIENT)
TATTOO MARKS (MODERN)
MASONS' MARKS (MEDIEVAL AND MODERN)
REMARKS
42
Gupte (1902)
Cunningham (1879)
43
Sarkar (in press)
Gorham (1911)
Sarkar (in press)

NO	SYMBOLS IN INSCRIPTIONS	GRAFFITI & SIGNS HARAPPAN	CHALCOLI-THIC	MEGALITHIC	MOTIFS ON POTTERY	SYMBOLS ON COINS	TATTOO MARKS (ANCIENT)	MASONS' MARKS (ANCIENT)	TATTOO MARKS (MODERN)	MASONS' MARKS (MEDIEVAL AND MODERN)	REMARKS
44	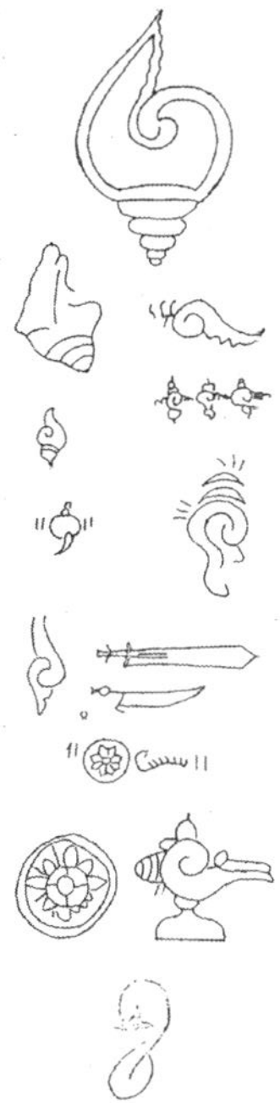										Gorham (1911)
45	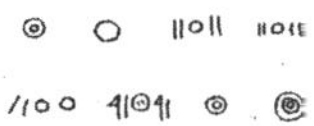					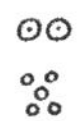		o		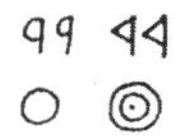	Sarkar (in press) Gorham (1911)
46		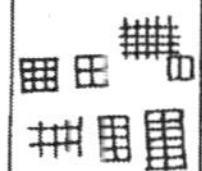	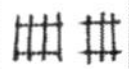	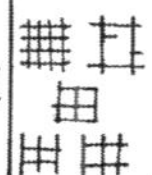							

NO	SYMBOLS IN INSCRIPTIONS	GRAFFITI & SIGNS: HARAPPAN	CHALCOLITHIC	MEGALITHIC	MOTIFS ON POTTERY	SYMBOLS ON COINS	TATTOO MARKS (ANCIENT)	MASONS' MARKS (ANCIENT)	TATTOO MARKS (MODERN)	MASONS' MARKS (MEDIEVAL AND MODERN)	REMARKS
47											Marshall (1951)
48											Gorham (1911)
49											
50											
51											
52											Rivett Carnac (1878)
53											
54											
55											
56											

NO	SYMBOLS IN INSCRIPTIONS	GRAFFITI & SIGNS: HARAPPAN	GRAFFITI & SIGNS: CHALCOLITHIC	GRAFFITI & SIGNS: MEGALITHIC	MOTIFS ON POTTERY	SYMBOLS COINS	TATTOO MARKS (ANCIENT)	MASONS' MARKS (ANCIENT)	TATTOO MARKS (MODERN)	MASONS' MARKS (MEDIEVAL AND MODERN)	REMARKS
57											
58										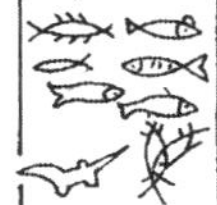	Rivett Carnac (1878)
59											
60	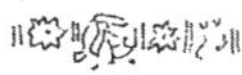										
61											
62											
63											
64					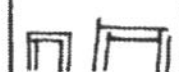						
65	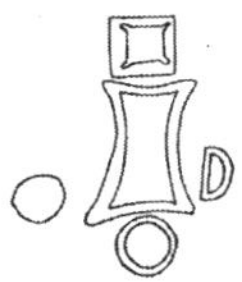					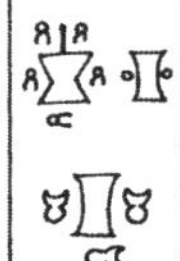					

NO	SYMBOLS IN INSCRIPTIONS	GRAFFITI & SIGNS			MOTIFS ON POTTERY	SYMBOLS ON COINS	TATTOO MARKS (ANCIENT)	MASONS' MARKS (ANCIENT)	TATTOO MARKS (MODERN)	MASONS' MARKS (MEDIEVAL AND MODERN)	REMARKS
		HARAPPAN	CHALCOLI-THIC	MEGALITHIC							
66											
67											
68											
69	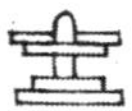										
70											Gorham (1911)
71											

PLATES

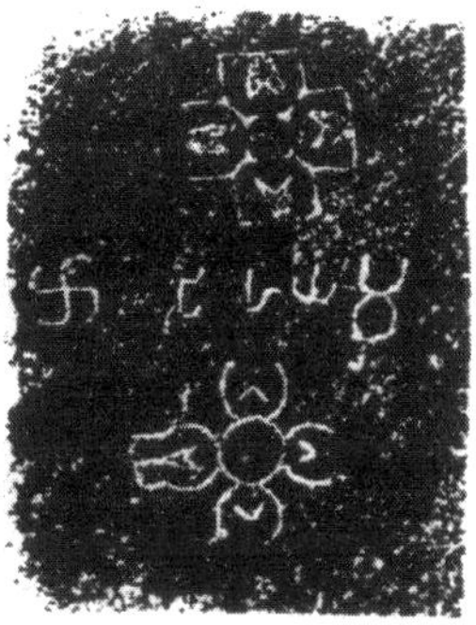

Pl. IA. Sanchi: early inscription reading *si ha ya* surrounded by four symbols

Pl. IB. Jankhat: inscription of Vīrasena with symbol on top

Pl. IC. Amaravati: early inscription with symbol at the end

Pl. ID. Udayagiri cave, Orissa: inscription with symbol at the beginning and the end

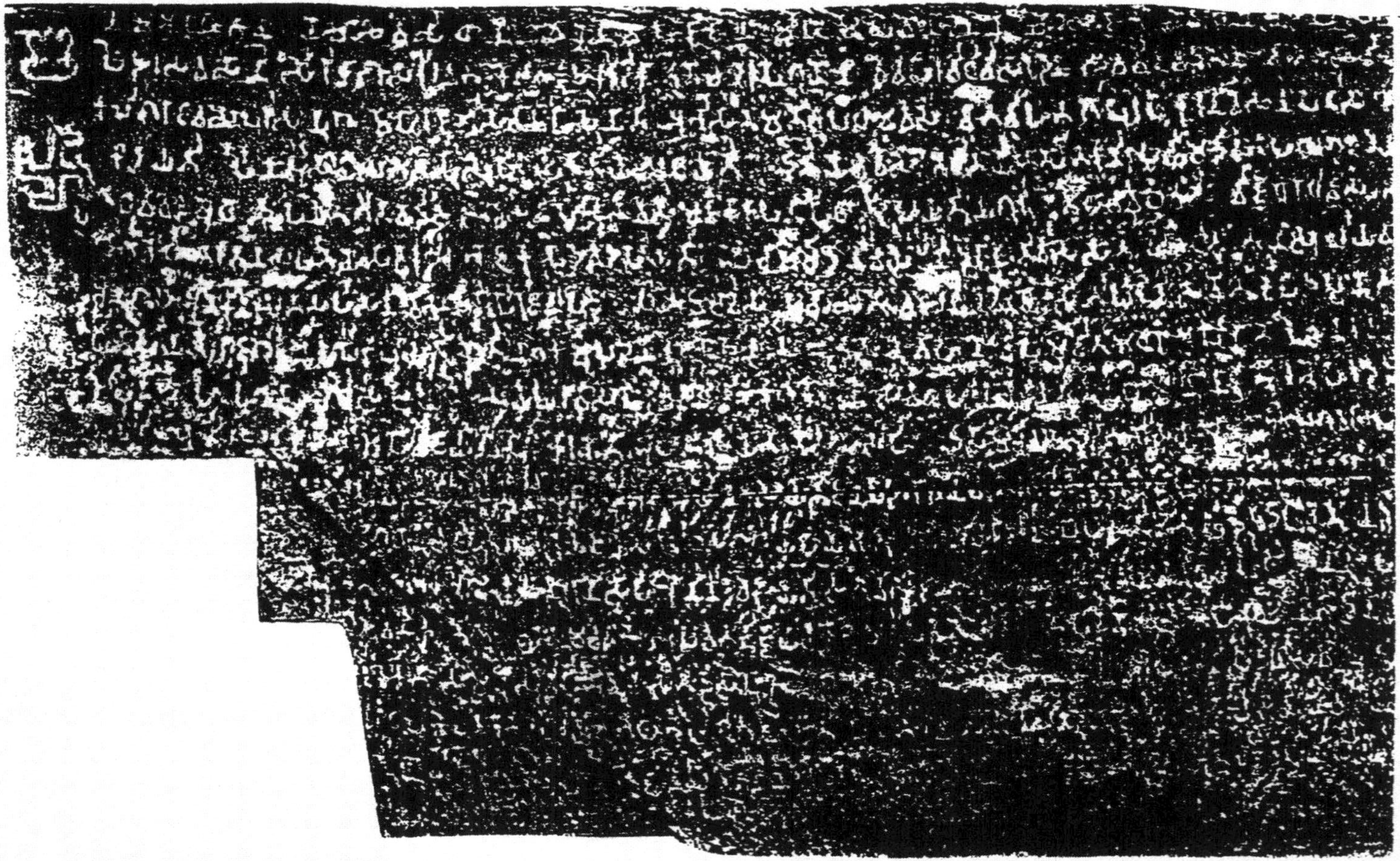

Pl. II. Hathigumpha: inscription of Khāravela with two symbols on the margin

Pl. III. Jaugada: Aśokan inscription with *svastika* and taurine symbols on top and middle

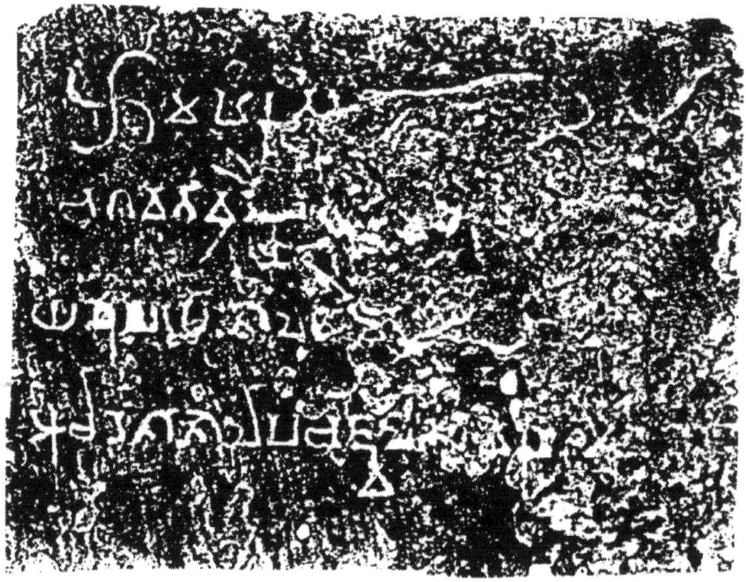

Pl. IVA. Mora (Mathura) well inscription with *svastika* at the beginning of the inscription

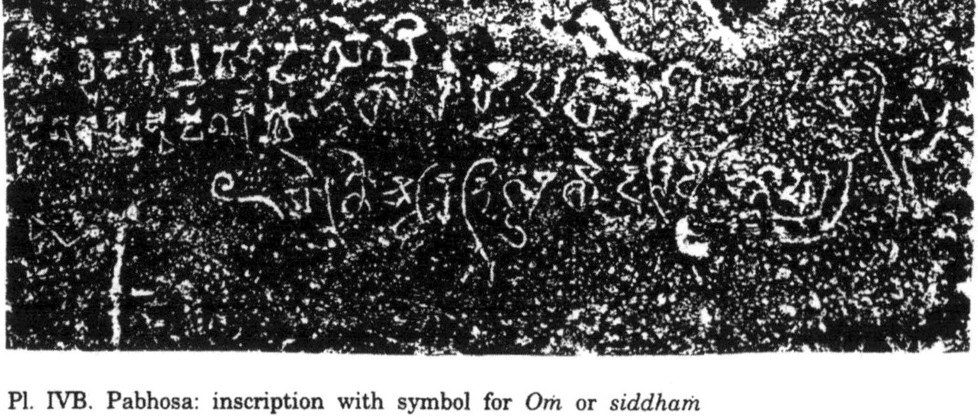

Pl. IVB. Pabhosa: inscription with symbol for *Oṁ* or *siddhaṁ*

Pl. V. Nachne-ki-Talai: inscription of Vyāghradeva with *chakra* in line 2

Pl. VI. Ganj: inscription of Vyāghradeva with *chakra* in line 1

Pl. VIIA. Inscription of Tejavarman with *śaṅkha*

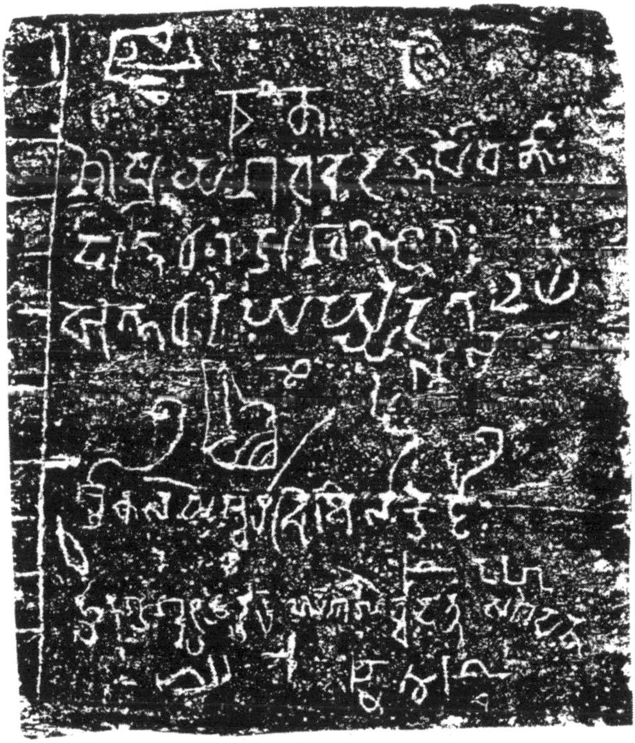

Pl. VIIB. Pabhosa: inscription on hermit's bed inside the cave with *śaṅkha* and another symbol

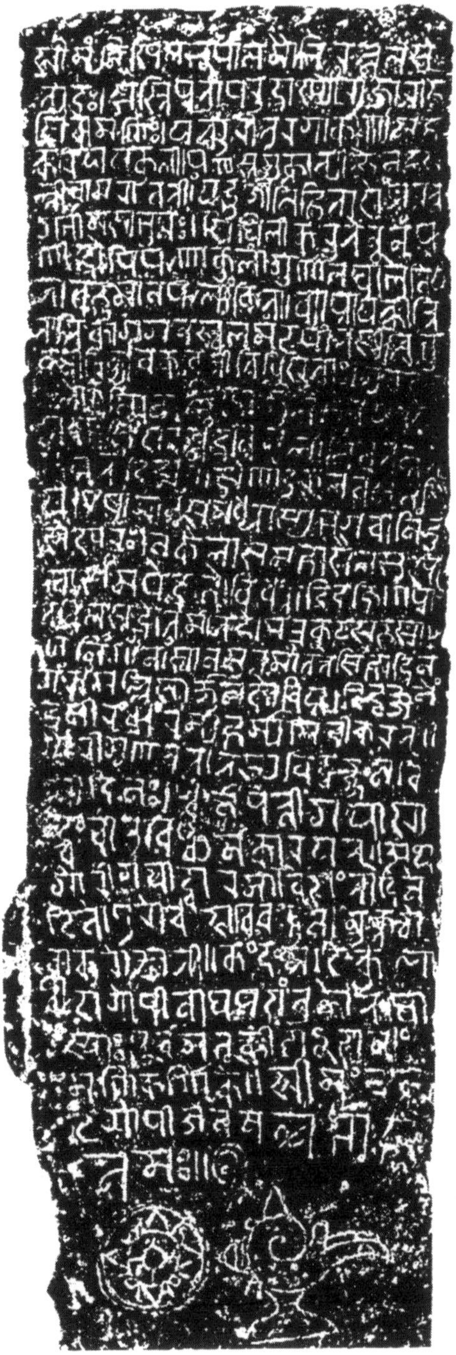

Pl. VIII. Gaya: inscription of the time of Kākatīya Pratāparudra I with *chakra* and *śaṅkha* at the end of the inscription

Pl. IX. Copper plate of Dhruva II of Gujarat Rāshṭrakūṭa Branch, Śaka 806 with endless knot sign

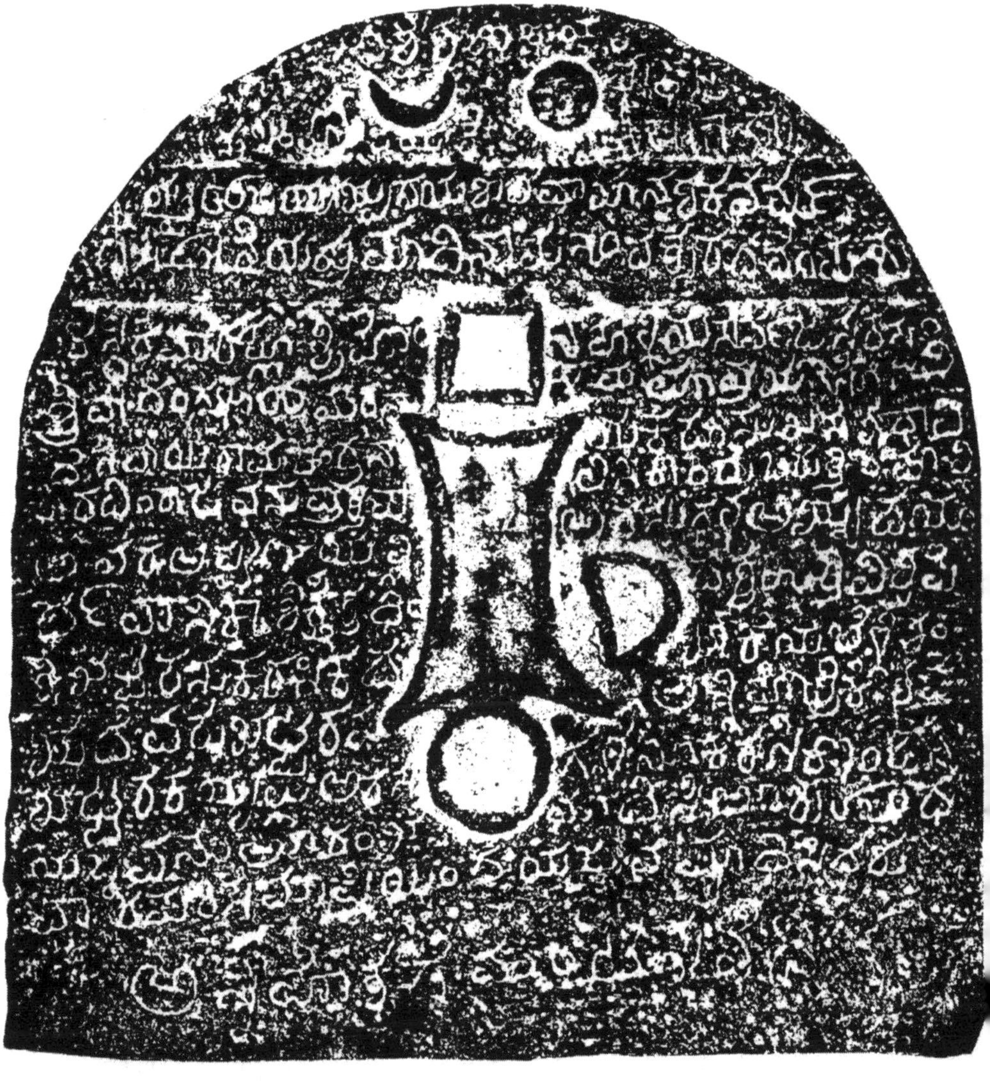

Pl. X. Sonda: sacrificial inscription with altar, etc. in the centre

Pl. XIA. Kalsi: engraved elephant figure with *gajatame* inscribed below

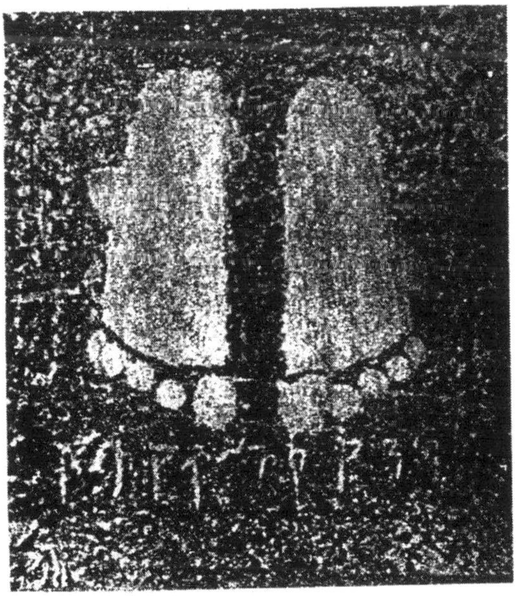

Pl. XIB. Tirath: Kharoshṭhī inscription with Buddha-*pāda*

Pl. XII. Ranganatha inscription of Sundara Pāṇḍya

Pl. XIII. Lucknow Museum plate of Kīrttipāla (front side) with the figure of Varāha on top

Pl. XIV. Lucknow Museum plate of Kīrttipāla (back side) with *śaṅkha* on top

Pl. XVA. Shakardarra: Kharoshṭhī inscription, dated year 40 with figure of donkey and pot

Pl. XVB. Rajapura copper plates of Madhurāntakadeva, Śaka 987, with imprecatory scene

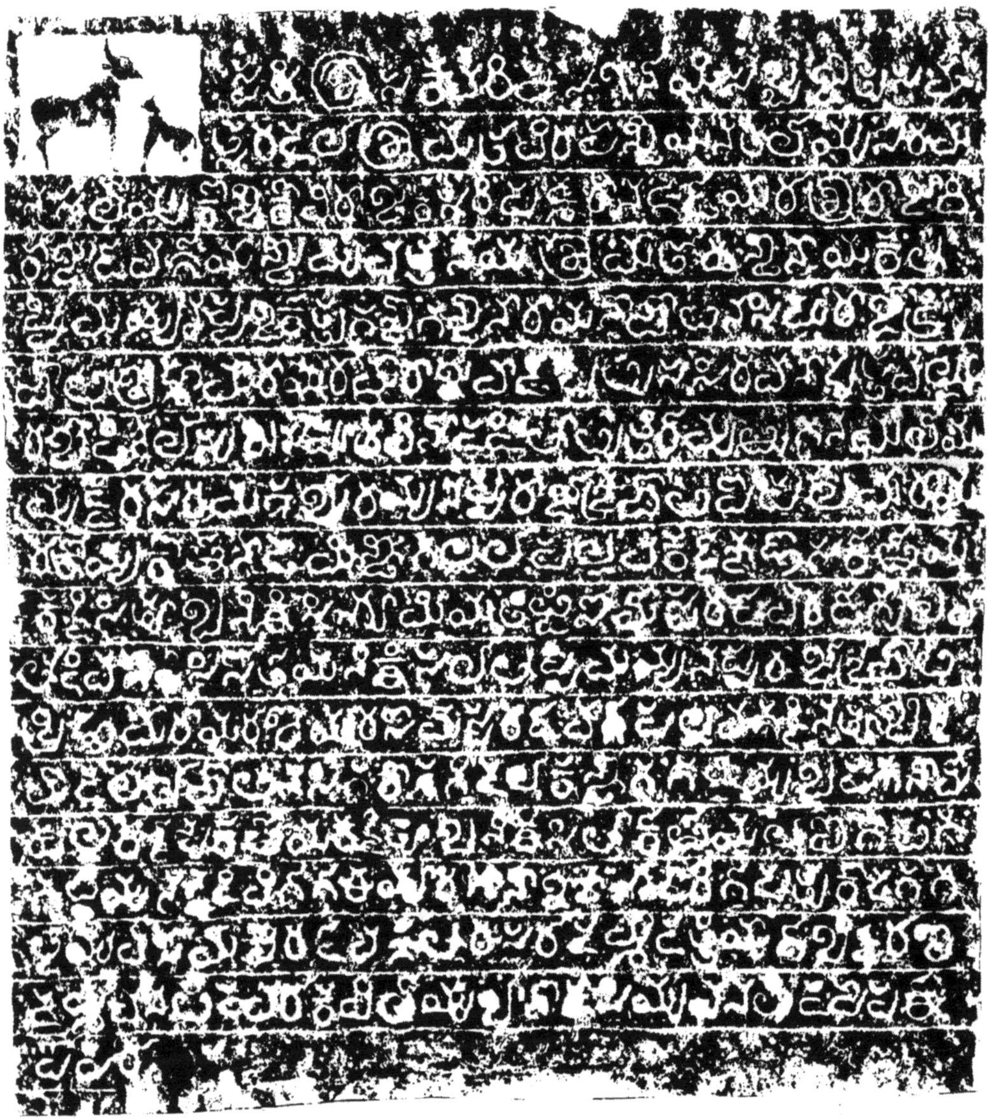

Pl. XVI. Mindigal inscription of Rājādhirāja, Śaka-Saṁvat 970, with figure of cow and calf in a corner at the beginning of the inscription

Pl. XVII. Narayanpal inscription of Guṇḍa-Mahādevī, AD 1111, with figures of a cow and calf, Śiva-*liṅga*, dagger, the sun and the moon

Pl. XVIII. Puratattva Sangrahalaya, Jabalpur: Brāhmī inscription. The figures on the proper left side of the record seem to be later than the inscription

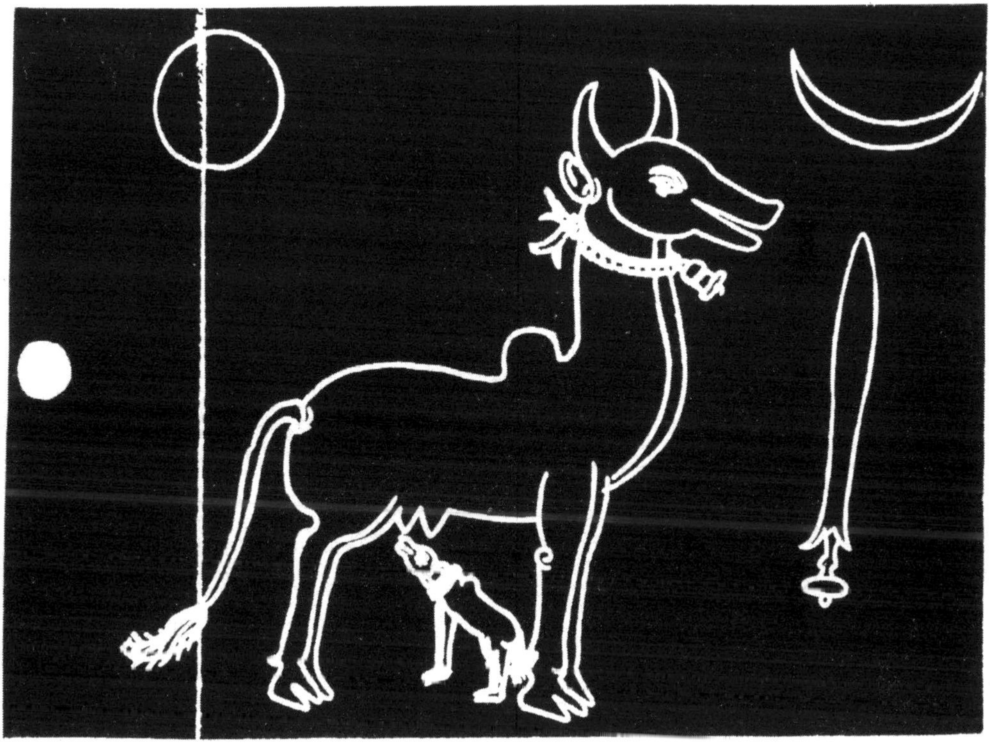

Pl. XIX. Talale plates of Gaṇḍarāditya, Śaka year 1032, with figure of a cow and suckling calf, a double-edged sword in upright position and the sun and the moon

Pl. XX. Miraj plates of Mārasiṁha, Śaka year 980, showing a squatting figure with folded hands, Śiva-*liṅga*, bull and the sun and the moon

SELECT BIBLIOGRAPHY

Leonhard Adam, *Primitive Art* (London, 1963).

Ekram Akurgal, *The Art of the Hittites* (London, 1962).

F.R. Allchin, 'Upon the contextual significance of certain groups of ancient Indian signs,' *Bulletin of the School of Oriental and African Studies,* University of London, Vol. XXII (1959), pp. 541-55.

J. Allan, *A Catalogue of the Indian Coins in the British Museum* (London, 1963).

Jitendra Nath Banerjea, *The Development of Hindu Iconography* (second edition, Calcutta, 1956).

Harold Bayley, *The Lost Language of Symbolism* (London, 1912).

S. Beal, 'The Swastika,' *The Indian Antiquary*, Vol. IX (1880), pp. 67-68.

Nalinikanta Bhattasali, 'Some image inscriptions from Bengal,' *Epigraphia Indica*, Vol. XVII (1923-24), pp. 349-62.

J.J. Boeles, 'The migration of the magic syllable Oṁ', *India Antiqua, A Volume of Oriental Studies presented by his friends and pupils to Jean Philippe Vögel, C.I.E.*, Kern Institute (Leyden, 1947), pp. 40-56.

G. Bühler, *Indian Palaeography* (reprinted, Calcutta, 1959).

Jas. Burgess, *Report on the Elura Cave Temples and the Brahmanical and Jaina Caves in Western India*, Archaeological Survey of Western India, Vol. V (London, 1883).

——, *Report on the Buddhist Cave Temples and their Inscriptions*, Archaeological Survey of Western India, Vol. IV (reprinted, Varanasi, 1964).

A.C. Burnell, *Elements of South-Indian Palaeography from the Fourth to the Seventeenth century AD* (London, 1878).

Ananda K. Coomaraswamy, *History of Indian and Indonesian Art* (London, 1927).

A. Cunningham, *The Stupa of Bharhut* (London, 1879).

A.H. Dani, *Indian Palaeography* (Oxford, 1963).

Harit Krishna Deb., 'The Svastika and the Oṁkāra', *Journal and Proceedings of the Asiatic Society of Bengal*, New Series, Vol. XVII (1921), pp. 231-44.

Durga Prasad, 'Classification and significance of the symbols on the Silver Punch-marked Coins of Ancient India', *Numismatic Supplement*, No. XLV (1934), pp. 60.

Durga Prasad, 'Observations on different types of Silver Punch-marked Coins, their Periods and Locale', *Numismatic Supplement*, No. XLVII (1937-38), Article no. 343, pp. 51-92.

Mircea Eliade, 'Methodological Remarks on the Study of Religious Symbolism,' in *The History of Religions*, edited by Mircea Eliade and Joseph M. Kitagawa (Chicago, 1959).

——, *Images and Symbols* (London, 1961).

G. Eliot Smith, *Elephants and Ethnologists* (London and New York, 1924).

Epigraphia Carnatica, Vol. XI.

Epigraphia India, Vols. I-XXXVII.

Arthur J. Evans, *Scripta Minoa*, Vol. I (Oxford, 1909).

H. Frankfort, *Cylinder Seals* (London, 1939).

Douglas Fraser, *The Many Faces of Primitive Art: A Critical Anthology* (New Jersey, 1966).

Sigmund Freud, *Totem and Taboo* (New York, 1946).

A. Ghosh and K.C. Panigrahi, 'Pottery of Ahichchhatra (U.P.),' *Ancient India*, No.1 (January, 1946), pp. 37-59.

——, 'Taxila (Sirkap) 1944-45,' *Ancient India*, No. 4 (July 1947- January 1948), pp. 41-85.

A. Ghosh and H. Sarkar, 'Beginnings of sculptural art in south-east India: a stele from Amaravati', *Ancient India*, Nos. 20 & 21 (1967), pp. 168-77.

Beatrice Laura Goff, *Symbols of Prehistoric Mesopotamia* (New Haven and London, 1963).

A. Gorham, *Indian Mason's Marks of the Moghul Dynasty* (London, 1911).

Parmeshwari Lal Gupta, *Punch-Marked Coins in the Andhra Pradesh Government Museum*, Andhra Pradesh Museum Series, No. 1 (Hyderabad, 1961).

B.A. Gupte, 'Notes on female tattoo-designs in India,' *The Indian Antiquary*, Vol. XXXI (1902), pp. 293-98.

——, 'Notes on female tattooing from Ootacamund,' *The Indian Antiquary*, Vol. XXXV (1906), pp. 269-70.

P.S. Handcock, *Archaeology of the Holy Land* (London, 1916).

E.W. Hopkins, *The Religions of India* (Boston, 1895).

E. Hultzsch, *Inscriptions of Aśoka*, Corpus Inscriptionum Indicarum, Vol. I (Oxford, 1925).

G.R. Hunter, *The Script of Harappa and Mohenjo-daro and its Connection with Other Scripts* (London, 1934).

Indian Archaeology — A Review.

Pandit Bhagvanlal Indraji, *Twenty-three Inscriptions from Nepal* (Bombay, 1885).

M.C. Joshi, 'Kuṇinda Coinage: A Review,' *Bharatiya Vidya*, Vol. XXII, Nos. 1-4 (1962), pp. 48-52.

M.C. Joshi and B.M. Pande, 'A newly-discovered inscription of Aśoka at Bahapur, Delhi', *Journal of the Royal Asiatic Society of Great Britain and Ireland*, Parts 3 & 4 (1967), pp. 96-98.

Carl G. Jung, *Man and His Symbols* (London, 1964).

V.E.G. Kenna, *Cretan Seals* (Oxford, 1960).

Sten Konow, *Kharoshṭhī Inscriptions*, Corpus Inscriptionum Indicarum, Vol. II, part I (Calcutta, 1929).

B.B. Lal, 'Excavations at Hastināpura and other Explorations in the Upper Gaṅga and Sutlej Basins', *Ancient India*, Nos. 10 & 11 (1954-55), pp. 5-151.

——, 'From the Megalithic to the Harappa: tracing back the graffiti on the pottery', *Ancient India*, No. 16 (1960), pp. 4-24.

C.E. Luard, 'Tattooing in Central India', *The Indian Antiquary*, Vol. XXXIII (1904), pp. 219 ff.

Earnest J.H. Mackay, *Further Excavations at Mohenjo-daro* (Delhi, 1938).

Donald A. Mackenzie, *The Migration of Symbols* (London, 1962).

Jacques Maritain, *Redeeming the Time* (London, 1943).

Sir John Marshall, *Mohenjo-daro and the Indus Civilization* (London, 1931).

——, *Taxila* (Cambridge, 1951).

Vasudev Vishṇu Mirashi, *Inscriptions of the Kalachuri-Chedi Era*, Corpus Inscriptionum Indicarum, Vol. IV (Ootacamund, 1955).

——, *Inscriptions of the Vākāṭakas*, Corpus Inscriptionum Indicarum, Vol. V. (Ootacamund, 1963).

H.G.M. Murray-Aynsley, 'Discursive Contributions towards the Comparative Study of Asiatic Symbolism', *The Indian Antiquary*, Vol. XV (1886), pp. 61ff.

Sarabhai Manilal Nawab, *Jaina Chitrakalpadruma* (in Gujarati) (Ahmedabad, 1936).

Gaurishankar Hirachand Ojha, *Bhāratīya Prāchīna Lipimālā* (in Hindi) (Ajmer, V.S. 1975).

Edward James Rapson, *Catalogue of the Coins of the Andhra Dynasty* (London, 1908).

Herbert Read, *The Meaning of Art* (Pelican Books, 1950).

H. Rivett-Carnac, 'Mason's marks from old buildings in the North-West Provinces of India', *The Indian Antiquary*, Vol. VII (1878), pp. 295-98.

Alan S.C. Ross, *The "Numeral Signs" of the Mohenjo-daro Script*, Memoirs of the Archaeological Survey of India, No. 57 (Delhi, 1938).

Chittaranjan Roy Chowdhary, *A Catalogue of Early Indian Coins in the Asuthosh Museum*, Part I (Calcutta, 1962).

Swami Sankarananda, *The Dictionary of Indian Hieroglyphs* (Calcutta, 1963).

H. Sarkar, *Studies in Early Buddhist Architecture of India* (New Delhi, 1966).

——, 'Mason's Mark from Nagarjunakonda,' *Suparna*, Vogel Commemoration Volume (in press).

H. Sarkar and B.N. Mishra, *Nagarjunakonda* (New Delhi, 1966).

R. Sewell, 'Notes on the *Swastika*,' *The Indian Antiquary*, Vol. X (1881), pp. 199-202.

R. Shamasastry, 'A theory of the origin of the Devanāgarī alphabet,' *The Indian Antiquary*, Vol. XXXV (1906), pp. 253 ff.

Y.D. Sharma, 'Exploration of Historical Sites', *Ancient India*, No. 9 (1953), pp. 116-69.

D.C. Sircar, 'Chidivalasa Plates of Devendravarman; Gaṅga Year 397', *Journal of the Asiatic Society of Bengal (Letters)*, Vol. XVIII (1952), pp. 77-81.

D.C. Sircar, *Indian Epigraphy* (Delhi, 1965).

——, *Select Inscriptions bearing on Indian History and Civilization*, Vol. I (second edition, Calcutta, 1965).

C. Sivaramamurti, *Amaravati Sculptures in the Madras Government Museum* (Madras, 1956).

Sidney Smith, *Early History of Assyria to 1000 BC* (London, 1928).

Vincent A. Smith, *The Jaina Stupa and other Antiquities of Mathura*, Archaeological Survey of India, New Imperial Series, Vol. XX, North-Western Provinces and Oudh, Vol. V, Muttra Antiquities (Allahabad, 1901).

P. Sreenivasachar, *A Corpus of Inscriptions in the Telingana Districts of H.E.H. The Nizam's Dominions*, Hyderabad Archaeological Series, No. 13 (Hyderabad, 1940).

P.R. Srinivasan, *Beginnings of the tradtions of South Indian Temple Architecture*, Bulletin of the Madras Government Museum, New Series—General Section, Vol. VII, No. 4 (Madras, 1959).

Aurel Stein, *An Archaeological Tour in Gedrosia*, Memoirs of the Archaeological Survey of India, No. 43 (Calcutta, 1931).

E. Thomas, 'The Swastika,' *The Indian Antiquary*, Vol. IX (1880), pp. 65-66.

R.L. Turner, *The Gavīmaṭh and Pālkīguṇḍu Inscriptions of Aśoka*, Hyderabad Archaeological Series, No. 10 (Hyderabad, 1952).

M.S. Vats, *Excavations at Harappa* (Delhi, 1940).

J. Ph. Vögel, *Antiquities of Chamba State*, Archaeological Survey of India, New Imperial Series, Vol. XXXVI, Part I (Calcutta, 1911).

M.J. Walhouse, 'Mason's Marks,' *The Indian Antiquary*, Vol. IV (1875), pp. 302-05.

——, 'Trojan and Indian prehistoric pottery and the Svastika symbol,' *The Indian Antiquary*, Vol. VII (1878), pp. 176-79.

E.H.C. Walsh, 'An examination of a find of Punch-Marked coins in Patna City, with reference to the subject of Punch-Marked coins Generally', *Journal of the Bihar and Orissa Research Society*, Vol. V, Part I (1919), pp. 16-72.

R.E.M. Wheeler, A. Ghosh and Krishna Deva, 'Arikamedu: An Indo-Roman trading station on the East Coast of India,' *Ancient India*, No. 2 (July, 1946), pp. 17-124.

Thomas Wilson, *The Swastika* (Washington, 1876).

Heinrich Zimmer, *The Art of Indian Asia*, Bolingen Series XXXIX (Pantheon Books, 1955).

INDEX